The
Best and Lightest

150 Healthy Recipes for Breakfast, Lunch and Dinner

by the editors of **FOOD NETWORK MAGAZINE**

clarkson potter/publishers
new york

Food Network Magazine

Editor in Chief Maile Carpenter
Creative Director Deirdre Koribanick
Managing Editor Maria Baugh
Food Director Liz Sgroi
Art Director Ian Doherty
Photo Director Alice Albert
Photo Editor Kathleen E. Bednarek
Designer Anthony Mikolajczyk
Copy Editors Joy Sanchez, Paula Sevenbergen
Senior Editor Yasmin Sabir
Senior Associate Food Editor Ariana R. Phillips
Associate Photo Editor Anna McKerrow
Photo Assistant Morgan Salyer
Assistant Managing Editor Heather DiBeneditto
Art Assistant Rachel Keaveny
Editorial Assistant Ana Rocha

Food Network Kitchen

Senior Vice President, Culinary Katherine Alford
Test Kitchen Director Claudia Sidoti
Recipe Developers Andrea Albin, Melissa Gaman
Bob Hoebee, Stephen Jackson, Amy Stevenson
Recipe Developer/Nutritionist Leah Trent Hope
Recipe Tester Vivian Chan

Hearst Communications

Editorial Director Ellen Levine
Vice President, Publisher Hearst Books
Jacqueline Deval
Creative Director, Content Extensions
Mark Gompertz
Product Manager
T.J. Mancini
Assistant Managing Editor
Kim Jaso

Library of Congress Cataloging-in-Publication Data is on file with the Library of Congress

A complete list of photography credits appears on page 336.

ISBN 978-0-8041-8534-9
eISBN 978-0-8041-8535-6

Printed in China

Cover design by Laura Palese
Cover photograph by Ryan Dausch
Cover food styling by Jamie Kimm

10 9 8 7 6 5 4 3 2 1

First Edition

TO YOUR HEALTH!

CONTENTS

SOUPS & STEWS

21 Kale and White Bean Soup

22 Spicy Chard Soup
V

25 Mexican Stew with Tilapia
GF

26 Low-Fat Clam Chowder
GF

29 Curried Chicken-Lentil Soup
GF

30 Chicken and Egg Soup with Pastina

33 Italian Wedding Soup

34 Vegetable Gumbo
V, VN

37 Ratatouille Soup
V

38 Ravioli and Vegetable Soup
V

41 Chickpea Chicken-Noodle Soup

42 Thai Dumpling Soup

45 Spanish Turkey Meatball Stew
GF

46 Slow-Cooker Sweet Potato–Lentil Soup
V, GF

49 Potato-Leek Soup with Bacon

50 Slow-Cooker Squash Stew
V, GF

SANDWICHES

57 Lentil Sloppy Joes

58 Chicken Dogs with Sweet Potato Fries

61 Indian Chicken Wraps

62 Asian Chicken Burgers

65 Spiced Burgers with Cucumber Yogurt

66 Tangy Meatloaf Burgers

69 Veggie Burger Pockets
V

70 Turkey-Avocado Sandwiches

73 Roast Beef Wraps with Dill Slaw

74 Steak and Hummus Sandwiches

77 Shrimp and Kale Pitas

78 Sardine Salad Sandwiches

POULTRY

85 Grilled Chicken Satay Salad
GF

86 Chicken with Arugula Pesto

89 Spicy Chicken Enchiladas
GF

90 Spiced Couscous and Chicken

93 Chicken Potpie

94 Grilled Chicken with Roasted Kale
GF

97 Chicken with Cacciatore Sauce
GF

98 Falafel Chicken with Hummus Slaw

101 Chicken Veracruz
GF

102 Chicken and Asparagus Crêpes

105 Spanish Chicken with Potato Roast
GF

106 Chicken Salad with Gazpacho Dressing

109 Honey-Mustard Chicken and Apples

110 Turkey Cutlets with Plum Salad
GF

113 Spicy Turkey Lettuce Cups

114 Turkey and Green Bean Stir-Fry

V= Vegetarian   **VN**= Vegan   **GF**= Gluten Free

Read labels carefully to avoid products with trace amounts of gluten.

MEAT

121 Steak Salad with Roasted Celery
GF

122 Grilled Steak with Barley Salad

125 Sweet-and-Spicy Mini Meatloaves

126 Sirloin with Teriyaki Broth

129 Chile-Rubbed Steak with Creamed Corn
GF

130 Lamb Steak with Olive Salsa
GF

133 Pork Tenderloin with Red Cabbage Slaw

134 Roasted Pork with Lentils and Squash

137 Sweet and Sour Pork Stir-Fry

138 Cold Asian Noodle Salad with Pork

141 Roasted Pork with Cajun Slaw
GF

142 Pork and Egg Lo Mein

145 Apple Pork Chops with Garlic Potatoes
GF

146 Pork Steaks with Zucchini Couscous

149 Pork and Wild Rice Salad
GF

150 Cajun Pork Chops with Kale and Beans
GF

153 Spaghetti Squash and Meatballs

FISH & SEAFOOD

EGGS, TOFU & BEANS

199 Feta-and-Cauliflower
Frittata
V, GF

200 Crustless Spinach
Quiche
V

203 Egg Foo Yong

204 Scrambled Eggs
with Broccolini
V

207 Polenta with Fontina
and Eggs
V, GF

208 Spaghetti Squash
Tostadas
V, GF

211 Middle Eastern
Rice and Lentils
V, GF

212 Eggplant and
Tofu Curry
V, VN, GF

215 Barbecue Tofu with
Cajun Rice
V, VN

216 Tofu-Potato Scramble
V

219 Tofu Tacos
V

220 Tofu-Vegetable
Stir-Fry
V, VN

V= Vegetarian   **VN**= Vegan   **GF**= Gluten Free

Read labels carefully to avoid products with trace amounts of gluten.

PASTA & GRAINS

227 Spaghetti with Tuna Marinara Sauce

228 Rigatoni with Spicy Shrimp

231 Broken Lasagna with Zucchini and Tomatoes
V

232 Low-Cal Fettuccine Alfredo
V

235 Sicilian Cauliflower Pasta
V

236 Gnocchi with Squash and Kale
V

239 Penne with Butternut Squash
V

240 Three-Cheese Macaroni
V

243 Penne with Turkey Ragu

244 Chinese Noodle–Vegetable Bowl
V, VN

247 Barley Risotto with Ham and Mushrooms

248 Ham and Black-Eyed Pea Salad

251 Quinoa and Bean Pilaf
V, GF

V= Vegetarian   **VN**= Vegan   **GF**= Gluten Free
Read labels carefully to avoid products with trace amounts of gluten.

SIDE DISHES

257 Bulgur Salad with Oranges and Olives
V, VN

258 Tuscan White Beans
V, GF

261 Super-Stuffed Baked Potatoes
GF

262 Roasted Carrots with Raisins and Walnuts
V, VN, GF

265 Kale and Pear Salad
V, VN, GF

266 Artichoke and Pea Gratin
V

269 Warm Beet-Orange Salad
V, VN, GF

270 Texas Black-Eyed Peas
GF

273 Carrot and Parsnip Fries
V

274 Broccoli with Walnut Romesco Sauce
V, VN, GF

277 Garden Potato Salad with Yogurt Dressing
V, GF

278 Low-Fat Scalloped Potatoes
V

281 Tropical Watercress Salad
V, VN, GF

282 Pickled Strawberry Salad
V, GF

285 Quinoa-Tomato Salad
V, VN, GF

286 Sesame-Ginger Snap Peas
V, VN, GF

289 Corn on the Cob with Basil Butter
V, GF

SWEETS

295 Low-Fat Cheesecake
V

296 Raspberry
Corn Muffins
V

299 Melon–Green Tea
Slushies
V, VN, GF

300 Oatmeal-Flax
Chocolate Chip Cookies
V

303 Low-Fat
Chocolate Pudding
V, GF

304 Strawberry
Corn Cakes
V

307 Mango-Chile Granita
V, VN, GF

308 Sweet Tofu-
Raspberry Strudel
V

311 Banana-Almond
Pudding
V

312 Coconut Macaroons
V, GF

315 Hot Peaches
and Cream
V, GF

316 Balsamic Strawberries
V, GF

319 Mango Sorbet with
Coconut Sauce
V, VN, GF

320 Cherry Couscous
Pudding
V

323 Broiled Apples
with Jam
V, GF

V= Vegetarian   **VN**= Vegan   **GF**= Gluten Free
Read labels carefully to avoid products with trace amounts of gluten.

Check out these fun snacks, too!

52 Veggie Chips
V, VN, GF

80 Pretzels
V

116 Mexican Dips
GF

154 Applesauce
V, VN, GF

194 Skewers

222 Ants on a Log

252 Crostini

290 Popcorn
V

324 Smoothies
V, GF

Acknowledgments

Every issue of *Food Network Magazine* is packed with healthful recipes created by the chefs in Food Network Kitchen, led by Katherine Alford and Claudia Sidoti. These chefs have an amazing ability to dream up dishes that are insanely delicious and also good for you—not easy!

Enormous thanks to our food director, Liz Sgroi, for taking the lead on this (and every) project and for being a never-ending source of creativity. Thanks to our managing editor, Maria Baugh, who always keeps us moving forward; to our copy editor, Joy Sanchez; and to Ellery Badcock and Hannah Kay Hunt for organizing so many recipes. Thanks to the Hearst Books team: Jacqueline Deval, vice president, publisher, and Mark Gompertz, creative director, content extensions. Thank you to our incredible partners at Clarkson Potter: Publisher Aaron Wehner, Associate Publisher Doris Cooper, Editor Angelin Borsics, Executive Director of Production Derek Gullino, Art Director Michael Nagin and Designer Sonia Persad.

We are so grateful to Creative Director Deirdre Koribanick—she created the fun, colorful, user-friendly look of the magazine, and she has brought the same energy and order to the pages of this book. Thanks to Photo Director Alice Albert and her team for producing the gorgeous images, to Kate Bednarek and Morgan Salyer for sourcing every photo, and to Ian Doherty and Anthony Mikolajczyk for perfecting every page.

We are also so thankful for the strong partnership that led to *Food Network Magazine*. Thanks to Food Network President Brooke Bailey Johnson, and at Hearst, President David Carey; President, Marketing and Publishing Director Michael Clinton; Executive Vice President and General Manager John P. Loughlin; and especially to our mentor, Editorial Director Ellen Levine.

Introduction

Believe it or not, the most difficult part about making this book was naming it. I know this sounds odd, considering the amount of work that went into creating 150 great-tasting healthful recipes. But every time we tried to come up with the book title, we were stumped. Words like "healthful" and "low-calorie" and "gluten-free" just don't sound like any fun. They don't sound like us, either; we're food lovers around here. I have never come home from work and pronounced, "Hey, kids, let's eat something healthful for dinner tonight!" And I've never hit that mid-afternoon slump and thought, "I can't wait to have a low-cal vegetarian taco." The food isn't the problem—these recipes are amazing. I just don't like the labels.

Not too long ago, a bunch of us at the magazine got together to talk about whether we should include more recipes for healthful food in each issue. It was one of the shortest meetings we've ever had: As we looked back, we realized that every issue was packed with good stuff—a big feature on roasting fall vegetables, a story about trendy grains, booklets full of chicken ideas, salad dressings, smoothies. The healthful recipes were all there. We just weren't being preachy about them. We were eating right, naturally.

What I love most about this book is that as you flip through it, you'd never know the food was good for you. The chefs in Food Network Kitchen are geniuses like that. French fries, potpies, sloppy joes, scalloped potatoes, mac and cheese—they're all in here, lightened up the right way, with smart ingredients and clever cooking techniques. (Trust me, we didn't cut calories by making the portions tiny!) Best of all, these dishes are delicious enough to serve by their proper names—without even mentioning the healthy part.

Maile Carpenter
Editor in Chief

SOUPS & STEWS

Kale and White Bean Soup

SERVES 4

ACTIVE: 20 min
TOTAL: 40 min

- 3 slices bacon, chopped
- 1 small onion, diced
- 3 carrots, cut into ½-inch pieces
- 2 cloves garlic, minced
- 1 tablespoon tomato paste
- ¾ teaspoon chopped fresh thyme
-   Kosher salt and freshly ground pepper
- 2 cups low-sodium chicken broth
- ½ cup grated parmesan cheese, plus 1 small piece rind
- 1½ cups small pasta, such as ditalini (about 8 ounces)
- 1 15-ounce can white beans, drained and rinsed
- 1 cup frozen chopped kale, thawed and squeezed dry

Keep a resealable plastic bag of cheese rinds in your freezer— they add great flavor to soups, and they last for up to a year.

1. Put the bacon in a large pot or Dutch oven over medium heat and cook, stirring occasionally, until crisp, about 4 minutes. Add the onion and cook, stirring occasionally, until slightly softened, about 3 minutes. Add the carrots, garlic, tomato paste, thyme and ½ teaspoon each salt and pepper and cook until the carrots begin softening, about 2 minutes. Add the chicken broth, 6 cups water and the parmesan rind. Increase the heat to high; cover and bring to a boil.

2. Add the pasta and beans and cook, uncovered, 5 minutes. Reduce the heat to medium and add the kale. Simmer, uncovered, until slightly thickened, about 7 minutes. Remove the parmesan rind, then stir in half of the grated cheese and season with salt and pepper. Ladle into bowls and top with the remaining cheese.

Per serving: Calories 499; Fat 16 g (Saturated 6 g); Cholesterol 44 mg; Sodium 763 mg; Carbohydrate 66 g; Fiber 9 g; Protein 23 g

Spicy Chard Soup

Vegetarian

SERVES 4

ACTIVE: 40 min

TOTAL: 40 min

- 2 bunches Swiss chard (about 2 pounds)
- 1 teaspoon caraway seeds
- 1 teaspoon cumin seeds
- 3 tablespoons extra-virgin olive oil, plus more for drizzling
- 1 medium onion, finely chopped
- 2 tablespoons tomato paste
- 1 tablespoon harissa or other chile paste
- 4 cloves garlic, finely chopped
- 6 cups low-sodium vegetable or chicken broth
- 1 lemon, halved

  Kosher salt
- ¼ cup plain Greek yogurt
- 4 hard-boiled eggs, peeled and quartered
- 2 cups pita chips, coarsely crushed

This soup gets its heat from harissa, a North African chile paste. Cool it down with a spoonful of lemony yogurt.

1. Cut the chard stems into ½-inch pieces and the leaves into 1-inch pieces; keep separate. Toast the caraway and cumin seeds in a skillet over medium heat, 1 to 2 minutes. Let cool, then grind in a spice grinder or transfer to a resealable plastic bag and crush with a heavy skillet.

2. Heat the olive oil in a large pot over medium heat. Add the chard stems and onion and cook until softened, 5 to 6 minutes. Clear a space in the pan, then add the tomato paste, harissa, garlic and ground spices. Cook 2 minutes, then stir into the vegetables. Add the chard leaves, chicken broth and 1 cup water, bring to a rapid simmer and cook until the chard is tender, about 10 minutes. Squeeze in the juice from ½ lemon and season with salt.

3. Mix the yogurt, the juice from the remaining ½ lemon and a pinch of salt in a small bowl. Divide the soup among bowls. Add the eggs, pita chips and a dollop of the yogurt mixture; drizzle with olive oil.

Per serving: Calories 315; Fat 19 g (Saturated 4 g); Cholesterol 255 mg; Sodium 866 mg; Carbohydrate 18 g; Fiber 5 g; Protein 20 g

Mexican Stew with Tilapia

Gluten-Free

SERVES 4

ACTIVE: 30 min

TOTAL: 30 min

- 4 6-ounce tilapia fillets, each cut into 4 pieces
- Kosher salt and freshly ground pepper
- 3 limes (2 juiced, 1 cut into wedges)
- ½ pound new potatoes, thickly sliced
- 4 small pieces frozen corn on the cob
- 2 tablespoons extra-virgin olive oil
- 1 large onion, finely chopped
- ½ teaspoon dried thyme
- 3 cloves garlic, minced
- 1 tablespoon ancho chile powder
- 1 bunch cilantro, leaves and tender stems coarsely chopped
- 1 15-ounce can no-salt-added diced fire-roasted tomatoes

We used ancho chile powder in this stew; it tastes rich and slightly sweet, and it's made of 100 percent ancho chiles. Standard chili powder is a blend of chiles and other spices.

1. Put the fish in a shallow dish and season with salt and pepper. Add the lime juice and toss; set aside. Put the potatoes in a saucepan, cover with water and season with salt. Bring to a boil; add the corn and cook, covered, until the vegetables are tender, about 8 minutes. Reserve 1 cup of the cooking water, then drain.

2. Meanwhile, heat the olive oil in a large skillet over medium-high heat. Add all but ⅓ cup of the chopped onion to the skillet along with the thyme and cook until soft, about 2 minutes. Add the garlic, chile powder and half of the cilantro and cook, stirring, 2 minutes. Add the tomatoes and cook, stirring occasionally, until slightly reduced, about 4 minutes. Add the potatoes, corn and reserved cooking water.

3. Add the fish and lime marinade to the skillet and simmer, spooning the sauce over the fish, until cooked through, about 5 minutes. Season with salt and pepper. Divide the stew among bowls and top with the remaining onion and cilantro. Serve with the lime wedges.

Per serving: Calories 381; Fat 10 g (Saturated 2 g); Cholesterol 85 mg; Sodium 333 mg; Carbohydrate 36 g; Fiber 5 g; Protein 39 g

Low-Fat Clam Chowder
Gluten-Free

SERVES 4

ACTIVE: 40 min

TOTAL: 1 hr 45 min

4 **pounds cherrystone clams, scrubbed**

2 **large red-skinned potatoes, peeled and cut into ½-inch cubes**

1 **slice lean center-cut bacon, chopped**

1 **medium onion, diced**

1 **stalk celery, thinly sliced**

2 **cloves garlic, minced**

1 **teaspoon fresh thyme**

2 **bay leaves**

1 **cup fat-free half-and-half**

  Kosher salt and freshly ground pepper

4 **teaspoons unsalted butter, sliced**

2 **tablespoons chopped fresh parsley**

2 **tablespoons chopped fresh chives**

½ **teaspoon paprika**

This soup has about 35 fewer grams of fat than the average clam chowder. We used a mix of pureed potatoes and fat-free half-and-half instead of the usual cream.

1. Put the clams and 2 cups water in a pot. Cover, bring to a boil over medium-high heat and cook 5 minutes. Uncover and continue cooking until the clams open, 5 to 10 minutes (discard any that do not open); transfer the clams to a bowl. Pour the liquid into a large measuring cup. (You should have 3 cups liquid; add water if needed.) Wipe out the pot.

2. Pour the liquid back into the pot through a paper towel–lined sieve. Add the potatoes, cover and simmer until tender, about 15 minutes. Remove one-third of the potatoes; set aside. Continue cooking the remaining potatoes, covered, until soft, about 10 more minutes. Puree in batches in a blender until smooth. Return the soup to the pot.

3. Cook the bacon in a skillet over medium heat until crisp, about 5 minutes. Add the onion and celery and cook until soft, about 5 minutes. Add the garlic, thyme and bay leaves and cook, stirring, about 3 more minutes. Add the bacon mixture and reserved potatoes to the soup. Cover and cook over low heat, about 5 minutes.

4. Meanwhile, remove the clams from their shells and roughly chop. Stir the clam meat and half-and-half into the soup; remove from the heat, cover and set aside, 20 to 30 minutes.

5. Discard the bay leaves. Season the soup with salt and pepper and reheat. Serve topped with a slice of butter, the parsley, chives and paprika.

Per serving: Calories 353; Fat 9 g (Saturated 4 g); Cholesterol 76 mg; Sodium 251 mg; Carbohydrate 36 g; Fiber 4 g; Protein 29 g

Curried Chicken-Lentil Soup

Gluten-Free

SERVES 4

ACTIVE: 20 min
TOTAL: 40 min

- 1 bunch scallions (white and light green parts only), chopped
- 1 jalapeño pepper, seeded and roughly chopped
- 2 ¼-inch-thick slices peeled ginger
- ½ cup fresh cilantro, plus more for topping
- 4 cloves garlic
- 3 cooking apples (such as McIntosh or Fuji), peeled and roughly chopped
- 2 teaspoons curry powder
- 1 13.5-ounce can light coconut milk
- Kosher salt
- 4 cups low-sodium chicken broth
- 1 cup dried red lentils, picked over and rinsed
- ½ pound skinless, boneless chicken breasts, cut into ¾-inch pieces
- Freshly ground pepper

We toasted the curry powder for a minute before adding the other ingredients; raw curry powder can taste harsh.

1. Combine the scallions, jalapeño, ginger, cilantro and garlic in a food processor and pulse until chopped. With the motor running, add the apples, a few pieces at a time, until chopped.

2. Cook the curry powder in a Dutch oven or large pot over medium-high heat, stirring, until lightly toasted, about 1 minute. Whisk in the coconut milk until smooth; cook until reduced by half, about 5 minutes. Add the apple-scallion mixture and ½ teaspoon salt. Cook, stirring, until thickened, about 5 more minutes.

3. Stir in the chicken broth and lentils. Bring to a boil, then reduce the heat to medium low and simmer until the lentils are tender and broken down, about 15 minutes. Add the chicken and simmer until cooked through, about 6 minutes. Season with salt and pepper; top with more cilantro.

Per serving: Calories 399; Fat 9 g (Saturated 6 g); Cholesterol 58 mg; Sodium 446 mg; Carbohydrate 50 g; Fiber 11 g; Protein 34 g

Chicken and Egg Soup with Pastina

SERVES 4

ACTIVE: 20 min
TOTAL: 35 min

¼ cup extra-virgin olive oil

1 small onion, finely chopped

Kosher salt and freshly ground pepper

½ 2½-to-3-pound rotisserie chicken (on the bone)

2 cups low-sodium chicken broth

Juice of 2 lemons

½ cup pastina or other small pasta

2 large eggs plus 2 egg yolks

2 cups baby spinach or other baby greens

¼ cup chopped fresh dill

¼ cup crumbled feta cheese, for topping

This soup gets its thick, creamy texture from eggs. To keep them from scrambling, gradually whisk hot broth into beaten eggs, then stir the warmed eggs into the soup.

1. Heat the olive oil in a large pot over high heat. Add the onion, 1 teaspoon salt, and pepper to taste; cook until the onion is slightly softened, about 5 minutes. Add the chicken, the broth, 4 cups water and the juice of 1 lemon; cover and bring to a boil. Reduce the heat to medium, add the pastina and simmer until the pasta is cooked and the soup is slightly thickened, about 15 minutes. Remove the chicken; when cool enough to handle, pull the meat off the bone and shred into bite-size pieces.

2. Remove the soup from the heat. Whisk the juice of the remaining lemon with the whole eggs and yolks in a medium bowl until frothy. Gradually whisk a ladleful of the hot soup into the egg mixture, then stir the warm egg mixture into the soup and return to medium-low heat. Cook until creamy, about 1 minute. Stir in the shredded chicken, spinach and dill, and season with salt and pepper. Ladle the soup into bowls; top with feta.

Per serving: Calories 385; Fat 24 g (Saturated 6 g); Cholesterol 271 mg; Sodium 942 mg; Carbohydrate 18 g; Fiber 1 g; Protein 24 g

Italian Wedding Soup

SERVES 4

ACTIVE: 30 min

TOTAL: 40 min

- 1 tablespoon extra-virgin olive oil
- 1 small onion, finely chopped
- 3 carrots, finely chopped
- 2 cloves garlic, finely chopped
- 2 teaspoons Worcestershire sauce
- 2 teaspoons chopped fresh sage
- 3 cups fat-free low-sodium chicken broth
- 1 tablespoon grated parmesan cheese, plus more for topping, and 1 piece rind
- ½ pound ground pork
- 3 tablespoons panko breadcrumbs
- ¾ cup orzo
- 8 ounces baby spinach (about 8 cups)

Spinach wilts almost instantly in hot liquids—especially the tender baby leaves. Add it to your soup at the last minute.

1. Heat the olive oil in a large pot over medium-high heat. Add the onion and carrots and cook, stirring, until slightly softened, about 4 minutes. Add half of the garlic and 1 teaspoon each Worcestershire sauce and sage; cook 1 minute. Add the chicken broth, 3 cups water and the parmesan rind and bring to a boil. Cover, reduce the heat to medium and simmer until the vegetables are tender, about 7 minutes.

2. Meanwhile, mix the pork, breadcrumbs, 1 tablespoon grated parmesan, the remaining garlic and the remaining 1 teaspoon each Worcestershire sauce and sage in a bowl. Form into 1-inch meatballs.

3. Increase the heat to medium high and bring the soup to a boil. Stir in the orzo and cook 6 minutes. Add the meatballs and cook until they are firm and float to the top, about 4 more minutes. Stir in the spinach and cook until wilted, about 1 more minute. Ladle the soup into bowls and top with parmesan.

Per serving: Calories 350; Fat 18 g (Saturated 6 g); Cholesterol 62 mg; Sodium 304 mg; Carbohydrate 29 g; Fiber 5 g; Protein 19 g

Vegetable Gumbo

Vegetarian | Vegan

SERVES 4

ACTIVE: 25 min
TOTAL: 40 min

3 tablespoons vegetable oil

3 tablespoons all-purpose flour

1 small onion, chopped

1 green bell pepper, chopped

2 stalks celery, chopped

3 cloves garlic, chopped

   Kosher salt and freshly
   ground pepper

1 tablespoon soy sauce

1 teaspoon smoked paprika
(preferably hot)

2 cups low-sodium vegetable
broth

1 pound kale or Swiss chard,
stemmed and chopped

1 10-ounce package frozen
black-eyed peas

   Brown rice, for serving
(optional)

Making a roux is an important technique in Southern cooking: You cook equal parts fat and flour and use that mixture to thicken soup, stews and sauces. It adds a nice toasty flavor.

1. Heat the vegetable oil in a large pot over medium-high heat. Add the flour and cook, stirring, until golden, about 3 minutes. Add the onion, bell pepper, celery, garlic, 3 tablespoons water and ¼ teaspoon each salt and pepper. Reduce the heat to medium, cover and cook, stirring occasionally, until the vegetables soften, about 8 minutes.

2. Add the soy sauce and paprika and cook, stirring, 30 seconds. Stir in the vegetable broth, scraping up any browned bits from the bottom of the pot, then cover and bring to a boil.

3. Add the greens and black-eyed peas to the pot. Reduce the heat, cover and simmer, stirring occasionally, until tender, about 15 minutes. Season with salt and pepper. Serve with rice.

Per serving (without rice): Calories 249; Fat 12 g (Saturated 1 g); Cholesterol 0 mg; Sodium 530 mg; Carbohydrate 32 g; Fiber 6 g; Protein 9 g

Ratatouille Soup

Vegetarian

SERVES 4

ACTIVE: 40 min
TOTAL: 40 min

- 3 tablespoons extra-virgin olive oil, plus more for brushing
- 1 large onion, diced
- 1 tablespoon herbes de Provence
  Kosher salt
- 1 small Japanese eggplant, diced
- 1 small zucchini, diced
- 1 yellow bell pepper, diced
- 1 28-ounce can whole San Marzano tomatoes, crushed
- 2 cups low-sodium vegetable or chicken broth
  Large handful of fresh basil leaves, torn
- 8 thick slices baguette
- 1 cup coarsely grated gruyère or Swiss cheese (about 4 ounces)
  Freshly ground pepper

If you don't have herbes de Provence in your spice cabinet, make your own: Combine two parts dried rosemary and one part each dried thyme and marjoram in a small jar.

1. Heat the olive oil in a large pot over medium-high heat. Add the onion and garlic and cook until soft, about 3 minutes. Add 1 to 2 teaspoons herbes de Provence and 1 teaspoon salt. Add the eggplant, zucchini and bell pepper and cook, stirring, 5 minutes. Add the tomatoes and their juices, the broth and half of the basil. Bring to a boil, then reduce the heat and simmer 20 minutes.

2. Preheat the broiler. Brush the bread with olive oil; sprinkle with the remaining 2 teaspoons herbes de Provence and salt to taste. Broil until lightly toasted. Top with the cheese, then continue broiling until melted.

3. Puree about half of the soup in a blender, then return to the pot. Season with salt and pepper. Ladle the soup into bowls and top with the cheese toast and the remaining basil.

Per serving: Calories 442; Fat 21 g (Saturated 7 g); Cholesterol 42 mg; Sodium 1,073 mg; Carbohydrate 44 g; Fiber 6 g; Protein 18 g

Ravioli and Vegetable Soup

Vegetarian

SERVES 4

ACTIVE: 20 min

TOTAL: 25 min

- 1 tablespoon extra-virgin olive oil
- 1 small onion, diced
- 3 medium carrots, halved lengthwise and sliced
- 3 stalks celery, sliced
- 1 teaspoon chopped fresh thyme
- 2 cups fat-free low-sodium vegetable or beef broth
- 1 9-ounce package small cheese ravioli
- 1 small head escarole, roughly chopped

  Kosher salt and freshly ground pepper
- 3 tablespoons grated parmesan cheese
- 8 slices whole-wheat baguette

Escarole is a slightly bitter leafy green that's loaded with vitamins A and K. It adds heft to this simple soup.

1. Heat the olive oil in a large pot over medium heat. Add the onion, carrots, celery and thyme and cook, stirring occasionally, until the vegetables begin softening, about 4 minutes. Add the broth and 3 cups water; increase the heat to high. Cover and bring to a boil, then add the ravioli. Reduce the heat to medium and simmer until the ravioli are tender (see label for approximate cooking time).

2. Add the escarole to the soup and cook, stirring, until wilted. Season with salt and pepper. Ladle the soup into bowls and sprinkle with the cheese. Serve with the bread.

Per serving: Calories 262; Fat 9 g (Saturated 3 g); Cholesterol 17 mg; Sodium 506 mg; Carbohydrate 34 g; Fiber 8 g; Protein 12 g

Chickpea Chicken-Noodle Soup

SERVES 4

ACTIVE: 20 min
TOTAL: 30 min

- 3 tablespoons extra-virgin olive oil
- 4 ounces spaghetti, broken into small pieces
- 1 carrot, thinly sliced
- 2 cloves garlic, chopped
- 1 teaspoon ground cumin
- ¼ teaspoon ground cinnamon
- ¾ cup chopped fresh cilantro
- 4 cups low-sodium chicken broth
- 1 15-ounce can chickpeas, drained and rinsed
- 1 15-ounce can diced tomatoes
- Kosher salt and freshly ground pepper
- 1 pound skinless, boneless chicken breasts, thinly sliced

Try toasting pasta before you make a noodle soup: Cook the dry pasta in oil until golden, then add the other ingredients. The toasted noodles will add a great nutty flavor.

1. Heat the olive oil in a large pot over medium-high heat. Add the spaghetti and cook, stirring, until lightly toasted, about 2 minutes. Add the carrot, garlic, cumin, cinnamon and half of the cilantro; cook, stirring, until the spices are toasted, about 1 minute. Add the chicken broth, chickpeas, diced tomatoes, 1 cup water, and salt and pepper to taste. Cover and bring to a simmer, then reduce the heat to medium low and cook until the spaghetti is just tender, about 8 more minutes.

2. Season the chicken with salt and pepper and add it to the soup. Simmer until cooked through, about 2 minutes. Add the remaining cilantro and season with salt and pepper.

Per serving: Calories 495; Fat 15 g (Saturated 2 g); Cholesterol 91 mg; Sodium 281 mg; Carbohydrate 45 g; Fiber 7 g; Protein 42 g

Thai Dumpling Soup

SERVES 4

ACTIVE: 25 min
TOTAL: 35 min

- 1 tablespoon vegetable oil
- 3 stalks celery, sliced
- 4 ounces shiitake mushrooms, stemmed and sliced
- 1 tablespoon curry powder
- 4 cups low-sodium chicken broth
- 1 cup coconut milk
- 1 tablespoon fish sauce, plus more to taste
- 4 ounces green beans, roughly chopped
- 1 red bell pepper, chopped
- 1 pound frozen Asian-style dumplings or pot stickers
  Juice of 1 lime, plus wedges for serving
  Kosher salt
  Sliced scallions, for topping

Coconut milk often separates in the can. Empty the liquid and solids into a bowl and whisk until smooth before you add it to the soup.

1. Heat the vegetable oil in a large pot over medium-high heat. Add the celery, mushrooms and curry powder; cook, stirring, until the curry powder is toasted, 1 to 2 minutes. Add the chicken broth, coconut milk, 1 tablespoon fish sauce and 1 cup water and bring to a simmer.

2. Add the green beans and bell pepper to the pot, reduce the heat to medium low and simmer until the vegetables are crisp-tender, about 3 minutes. Add the dumplings and cook until tender, about 4 minutes. Stir in the lime juice. Season the soup with salt and add more fish sauce to taste. Top with sliced scallions and serve with lime wedges.

Per serving: Calories 400; Fat 26 g (Saturated 15 g); Cholesterol 50 mg; Sodium 914 mg; Carbohydrate 28 g; Fiber 5 g; Protein 18 g

Spanish Turkey Meatball Stew
Gluten-Free

SERVES 4

ACTIVE: 30 min
TOTAL: 35 min

- 2 tablespoons extra-virgin olive oil
- 1 large onion, chopped
- 5 cloves garlic, minced
  Kosher salt
- 1 teaspoon smoked paprika
- 1 cup sliced small carrots
- 2 14-ounce cans low-sodium diced fire-roasted tomatoes
- 2 cups low-sodium chicken broth
- 1 15-ounce can chickpeas, drained and rinsed
- 1¼ pounds lean ground turkey
- ¾ cup fresh parsley, chopped, plus more for topping
  Freshly ground pepper

Instead of browning meatballs in oil, cook them right in a sauce or stew. They'll absorb tons of flavor.

1. Heat the olive oil in a large skillet over medium-high heat. Add the onion, garlic and a pinch of salt and cook, stirring occasionally, until soft, about 5 minutes. Transfer half of the mixture to a large bowl.

2. Add the paprika and carrots to the remaining onion mixture in the skillet and cook 1 minute. Add the tomatoes, chicken broth and chickpeas; bring to a rapid simmer and cook, stirring occasionally, until slightly thickened, about 6 minutes.

3. Meanwhile, add the ground turkey, parsley, 1 teaspoon salt and ¼ teaspoon pepper to the bowl with the reserved onion mixture and mix with your hands. Form the turkey mixture into about 20 meatballs. Place the meatballs in the skillet with the tomato mixture and simmer, turning once, until cooked through, about 7 minutes. Season with pepper and top with parsley.

Per serving: Calories 458; Fat 18 g (Saturated 4 g); Cholesterol 81 mg; Sodium 1,234 mg; Carbohydrate 36 g; Fiber 8 g; Protein 38 g

Slow-Cooker Sweet Potato–Lentil Soup

Vegetarian | Gluten-Free

SERVES 4

ACTIVE: 25 min

TOTAL: 8 hr 25 min

- 1 large sweet potato, peeled and diced
- 3 medium carrots, cut into ½-inch pieces
- 3 stalks celery, cut into ½-inch pieces
- 2 leeks (white and light green parts only), halved lengthwise and cut into ½-inch pieces
- ¾ cup dried yellow or red lentils, picked over and rinsed
- 1 4-inch piece ginger, peeled and finely grated
- 1 teaspoon curry powder
  Kosher salt
- 1 tablespoon unsalted butter
- 2 cloves garlic, thinly sliced
  Juice of ½ lemon
- ½ cup chopped fresh cilantro

Sweet potatoes are packed with fiber, potassium and vitamin A— and they cook perfectly in the slow cooker.

1. Combine the sweet potato, carrots, celery, leeks, lentils, ginger, ¾ teaspoon curry powder and 1 teaspoon salt in a 4-to-6-quart slow cooker. Add 6 cups water and stir, then cover and cook on low, undisturbed, 8 hours.

2. Stir the soup vigorously with a whisk to make a rough puree. Thin with hot water, if desired.

3. Melt the butter in a small skillet over medium-high heat. Add the garlic and the remaining ¼ teaspoon curry powder and cook until the curry powder is slightly toasted, about 1 minute. Stir the curry mixture into the soup and add the lemon juice, cilantro, and salt to taste.

Per serving: Calories 257; Fat 4 g (Saturated 2 g); Cholesterol 8 mg; Sodium 580 mg; Carbohydrate 45 g; Fiber 10 g; Protein 12 g

Potato-Leek Soup with Bacon

SERVES 4

ACTIVE: 40 min
TOTAL: 40 min

- 2 tablespoons unsalted butter
- ½ teaspoon smoked paprika
- 1½ cups cubed crusty bread
- 4 slices bacon, chopped
- 2 large leeks (white and light green parts only), thinly sliced
- 2 cloves garlic, chopped
- 4 cups low-sodium chicken broth
- 2 medium russet potatoes, peeled and cut into ½-inch pieces
- Kosher salt and freshly ground pepper
- ½ cup heavy cream
- 1½ cups frozen peas (do not thaw)
- ¼ cup chopped fresh parsley

Make smoked paprika your secret ingredient: It brings out the flavor of the bacon without adding extra fat.

1. Preheat the oven to 400°. Make the croutons: Melt 1 tablespoon butter, then mix with the paprika in a bowl. Add the bread cubes and toss. Spread on a baking sheet and bake until golden, 8 to 10 minutes.

2. Meanwhile, cook the bacon in a large saucepan over medium heat until crisp, about 8 minutes. Transfer with a slotted spoon to a paper towel–lined plate. Discard all but about 1 tablespoon fat from the pan. Add the remaining 1 tablespoon butter, then add the leeks and garlic; cover and cook until soft, about 5 minutes. Add the chicken broth, 2 cups water, the potatoes and ¼ teaspoon each salt and pepper; cover and bring to a boil over high heat. Reduce the heat to medium and simmer, partially covered, until the potatoes are tender, about 10 minutes.

3. Puree half of the soup in a blender (remove the filler cap to let steam escape), then return to the pot. Add the cream and bring to a simmer. Add the peas and cook until tender, about 3 minutes. Season with salt and pepper. Serve topped with the croutons, bacon and parsley.

Per serving: Calories 446; Fat 25 g (Saturated 13 g); Cholesterol 91 mg; Sodium 555 mg; Carbohydrate 42 g; Fiber 6 g; Protein 15 g

Slow-Cooker Squash Stew

Vegetarian | Gluten-Free

SERVES 4

ACTIVE: 25 min

TOTAL: 8 hr 35 min

- 3 tablespoons extra-virgin olive oil
- 1 medium onion, thinly sliced
- 2 cloves garlic, sliced
- 2 tablespoons tomato paste
- ¼ teaspoon red pepper flakes
- 1½ cups dried chickpeas, rinsed
- 1 pound butternut squash, peeled and cut into large pieces
- 1 bunch Swiss chard, leaves and stems separated and roughly chopped
- 1 piece parmesan cheese rind, plus grated parmesan for topping (optional)

  Kosher salt and freshly ground pepper

  Crusty bread, for serving (optional)

Dried beans hold up well in a slow cooker: They soften but still keep their shape. Canned beans can get mushy.

1. Heat the olive oil in a large skillet over medium-high heat. Add the onion and garlic and cook until the onion is soft and golden brown, 4 to 5 minutes. Stir in the tomato paste and red pepper flakes and cook 1 minute. Stir in ½ cup water, scraping up any browned bits. Transfer the contents of the skillet to a 6-quart slow cooker.

2. Add the chickpeas, squash, chard stems (not the leaves), the parmesan rind, 2 teaspoons salt and 7 cups water to the slow cooker. Stir, then cover and cook on low, 8 hours.

3. Just before serving, lift the lid and stir in the chard leaves; cover and continue cooking 10 more minutes. Season with salt and pepper and stir to slightly break up the squash. Discard the parmesan rind. Ladle the stew into bowls; top with grated parmesan and serve with bread.

Per serving: Calories 428; Fat 15 g (Saturated 2 g); Cholesterol 0 mg; Sodium 1,250 mg; Carbohydrate 63 g; Fiber 17 g; Protein 18 g

RED CABBAGE CHIPS

Cut away any large white ribs from 8 red cabbage leaves. Tear the leaves into 1½-inch pieces. Working in batches, arrange the cabbage pieces in a single layer on a flat microwave-safe plate coated with cooking spray. Mist with cooking spray, then sprinkle with salt and mustard powder. Microwave until slightly browned, about 5 minutes. Transfer the chips to a rack to cool. If they're still soft, microwave 30 more seconds.

EGGPLANT CHIPS

Line a baking sheet with a silicone mat; coat generously with cooking spray. Slice a firm Japanese eggplant ¹⁄₁₆ to ⅛ inch thick using a mandoline. Arrange on the baking sheet in a single layer; coat with cooking spray and sprinkle with salt. Bake at 250°, 50 minutes, rotating the baking sheet halfway through. Flip the slices; continue baking until browned, 20 more minutes. Transfer the chips to a rack to cool.

ZUCCHINI CHIPS

Line a baking sheet with a silicone mat; coat generously with cooking spray. Slice 1 small zucchini 1/16 to 1/8 inch thick using a mandoline. Arrange on the baking sheet in a single layer; coat with cooking spray and sprinkle with salt. Bake at 250°, 50 minutes, rotating the baking sheet halfway through. Flip the slices; continue baking until browned, 30 to 40 more minutes. Transfer the chips to a rack to cool.

TOMATO CHIPS

Slice 1 tomato about 1/16 inch thick with a serrated knife; pat dry with paper towels (discard the end pieces). Sprinkle with salt and let sit 15 minutes, then blot dry with paper towels. Arrange in a single layer on a flat microwave-safe plate coated with cooking spray. Mist with cooking spray, then microwave until they start drying out, about 6 minutes. Carefully flip; microwave until stiff and mostly dry, 30 seconds to 1 minute. Transfer the chips to a rack to cool.

ACORN SQUASH CHIPS

Line 2 baking sheets with silicone mats. Quarter 1 acorn squash and scoop out the seeds. Slice the squash quarters crosswise about 1/16 inch thick using a mandoline. Drizzle with olive oil and toss; arrange on the baking sheets in a single layer and sprinkle with salt. Bake at 250°, 50 minutes, rotating the baking sheets halfway through. Flip the slices and continue baking until browned, about 15 more minutes. Transfer the chips to a rack to cool.

SANDWICHES

Lentil Sloppy Joes

SERVES 6

ACTIVE: 30 min
TOTAL: 1 hr 10 min

- 2 tablespoons vegetable oil
- ½ small onion, finely chopped
- 1 small carrot, finely chopped
- ½ bell pepper (red or green), finely chopped
- ½ cup ketchup
- 1 clove garlic, finely chopped
- ½ cup dried brown lentils, picked over and rinsed
- ¼ teaspoon dried oregano
- Kosher salt and freshly ground pepper
- 8 ounces ground beef
- 1 tablespoon Worcestershire sauce
- 6 whole-wheat hamburger buns, toasted
- 6 slices cheddar cheese
- Sliced pickles and/or pickled jalapeño peppers, for topping (optional)

To lighten up the classic sloppy joe, we used lentils in place of some beef. The lentils taste meaty but add almost no fat.

1. Heat 1 tablespoon vegetable oil in a medium saucepan over medium-high heat. Add the onion, carrot, bell pepper and 2 tablespoons ketchup and cook, stirring occasionally, until the vegetables are slightly soft, about 3 minutes. Add the garlic and cook, stirring, 30 seconds. Add the lentils, oregano and 4 cups water; bring to a boil and cook 5 minutes, then reduce the heat to medium low and simmer until the lentils are tender and the water is absorbed, 35 to 40 minutes (add up to 1 more cup water if necessary). Season with salt and pepper.

2. Heat the remaining 1 tablespoon vegetable oil in a large nonstick skillet over medium-high heat. Add the beef and cook, breaking it up with a spoon, until it starts browning, about 2 minutes. Add the Worcestershire sauce and the remaining 6 tablespoons ketchup and cook, stirring, until combined. Add the lentil mixture and 1 cup water and cook, stirring occasionally, until the lentils are soft and the mixture thickens, about 8 minutes. Season with salt and pepper.

3. Fill the buns with the cheese and lentil mixture. Top with pickles and/or pickled jalapeños.

Per serving: Calories 404; Fat 18 g (Saturated 8 g); Cholesterol 53 mg; Sodium 669 mg; Carbohydrate 40 g; Fiber 6 g; Protein 23 g

Chicken Dogs with Sweet Potato Fries

SERVES 4

ACTIVE: 30 min
TOTAL: 40 min

FOR THE FRIES

- ½ cup panko breadcrumbs
- 1 teaspoon ground cumin
- 1 teaspoon paprika
- 1 tablespoon extra-virgin olive oil

  Kosher salt
- 1 large egg white
- 2 medium sweet potatoes, peeled and cut into ¼-inch-thick sticks

FOR THE HOT DOGS

- 2 ears of corn, husked
- ¼ cup chopped seedless cucumber
- ¼ cup chopped orange bell pepper

  Juice of 1 lime
- 1 teaspoon sugar

  Kosher salt
- 2 tablespoons chopped fresh basil
- 1 tablespoon extra-virgin olive oil
- 4 chicken hot dogs
- 2 tablespoons barbecue sauce, plus more for dipping
- 4 potato hot dog buns, split and toasted

Baked fries can taste almost as good as the real thing. The trick: Dip the potatoes in beaten egg whites before baking: The egg whites dry out in the oven and make the fries extra crisp.

1. Make the fries: Put a baking sheet in the oven and preheat to 425°. Combine the panko, cumin, paprika, olive oil and 1 teaspoon salt in a bowl.

2. Whisk the egg white in a medium bowl until frothy. Add the sweet potatoes and toss until coated, then add the panko mixture and toss. Spread the sweet potatoes on the hot baking sheet and sprinkle with any remaining crumbs from the bowl. Bake until the fries are tender and crisp, about 25 minutes.

3. Meanwhile, prepare the hot dogs: Preheat a grill to medium high. Grill the corn, turning occasionally, until slightly charred, about 6 minutes; let cool. Cut the kernels off the cobs and toss with the cucumber, bell pepper, lime juice, sugar and ¼ teaspoon salt in a bowl. Stir in the basil and olive oil.

4. Grill the hot dogs, turning occasionally and brushing with the barbecue sauce, until marked, about 5 minutes. Put the hot dogs in the buns and top with the corn mixture. Serve with the fries and barbecue sauce for dipping.

Per serving: Calories 474; Fat 22 g (Saturated 6 g); Cholesterol 35 mg; Sodium 1,431 mg; Carbohydrate 54 g; Fiber 5 g; Protein 16 g

Indian Chicken Wraps

SERVES 4

ACTIVE: 25 min
TOTAL: 25 min

1 1-inch piece ginger, peeled

1 serrano chile pepper, halved, seeded and roughly chopped

½ small onion, roughly chopped

½ teaspoon ground cumin

   Kosher salt

½ cup low-fat plain yogurt

2 teaspoons fresh lime juice

⅓ cup chopped fresh cilantro

1 tablespoon vegetable oil

2 cups shredded rotisserie chicken (skin removed)

2 medium carrots, shredded

4 pieces naan bread or pocketless pita, warmed

   Potato chips, for serving (optional)

Fresh ginger adds a spicy kick to these wraps. To peel the knobby root, scrape off the skin with the tip of a spoon.

1. Combine the ginger, chile, onion, cumin and ¼ teaspoon salt in a mini food processor and pulse to make a thick paste. (Or finely chop and mash with the flat side of a knife.) Mix the yogurt, lime juice, cilantro and a pinch of salt in a bowl. Cover and chill until ready to use.

2. Heat the vegetable oil in a large skillet over medium-high heat. Add the ginger-chile paste and cook, stirring, until most of the liquid has evaporated and the mixture is slightly toasted, about 5 minutes. Stir in the chicken, carrots, ¼ teaspoon salt and ½ cup water and continue to cook, stirring, until the sauce is thick and the chicken is heated through, about 2 more minutes. Season with salt.

3. Spoon one-quarter of the chicken filling down the middle of each piece of bread. Drizzle with some of the yogurt sauce and roll up. Serve with chips.

Per serving (without chips): Calories 483; Fat 19 g (Saturated 5 g); Cholesterol 115 mg; Sodium 955 mg; Carbohydrate 43 g; Fiber 5 g; Protein 37 g

Asian Chicken Burgers

SERVES 4

ACTIVE: 15 min
TOTAL: 30 min

Cooking spray
1 small carrot
1 small red onion, halved
1 pound ground chicken
¼ cup panko breadcrumbs
¼ cup hoisin sauce
1 tablespoon grated peeled ginger
4 teaspoons low-sodium soy sauce
3 teaspoons hot Asian chile sauce, such as sambal oelek
8 ounces white mushrooms, thinly sliced
2 teaspoons toasted sesame oil
Juice of 1 lime
4 whole-wheat sesame hamburger buns

Sneak a grated carrot into burgers, meatballs or meatloaf. The carrot adds a little sweetness as well as extra moisture.

1. Preheat the oven to 375°. Mist a baking sheet with cooking spray. Grate the carrot and ½ onion into a large bowl. Add the chicken, panko, 2 tablespoons hoisin sauce, the ginger, 3 teaspoons soy sauce and 1 teaspoon chile sauce and mix until combined. Shape the chicken mixture into 4 patties and place on the prepared baking sheet. Bake until cooked through, about 20 minutes.

2. Meanwhile, thinly slice the remaining ½ onion. Toss with the mushrooms, sesame oil, lime juice and the remaining 1 teaspoon soy sauce in a bowl. Mix the remaining 2 tablespoons hoisin sauce and 2 teaspoons chile sauce with 1 tablespoon water in another bowl.

3. Warm the hamburger buns in the oven. Serve the burgers on the buns with a drizzle of the hoisin-chile sauce and some of the mushroom mixture.

Per serving: Calories 360; Fat 14 g (Saturated 3 g); Cholesterol 75 mg; Sodium 1,143 mg; Carbohydrate 40 g; Fiber 4 g; Protein 24 g

Spiced Burgers with Cucumber Yogurt

SERVES 4

ACTIVE: 25 min
TOTAL: 25 min

½ seedless cucumber, peeled and finely chopped

½ cup low-fat plain Greek yogurt

1 tablespoon chopped fresh cilantro

Kosher salt and freshly ground pepper

1¼ pounds 90% lean ground beef

¼ cup finely chopped red onion

1 clove garlic, finely grated

1½ teaspoons curry powder

1 tablespoon extra-virgin olive oil

4 sesame hamburger buns, split and toasted

Sweet potato chips, for serving (optional)

Pickled okra or other pickled vegetables, for serving (optional)

We topped these curry-spiced burgers with raita, a classic Indian condiment made with yogurt and cucumber. Make a double batch and try it with the eggplant curry on page 212.

1. Mix the cucumber, yogurt, cilantro, ½ teaspoon salt, and pepper to taste in a bowl. Set aside while you make the burgers.

2. Combine the ground beef, onion, garlic, curry powder, ½ teaspoon salt and ⅛ teaspoon pepper in a bowl and mix with your hands until just combined. Form into four 4-inch-wide patties, about ½ inch thick.

3. Heat the olive oil in a large cast-iron skillet over medium-high heat. Add the patties and cook, turning once, until cooked through, 7 to 8 minutes for medium.

4. Place the burgers on the buns. Stir the cucumber-yogurt mixture and spoon on top. Serve the burgers with sweet potato chips and pickled okra.

Per serving (without chips): Calories 428; Fat 23 g (Saturated 8 g); Cholesterol 80 mg; Sodium 765 mg; Carbohydrate 25 g; Fiber 2 g; Protein 30 g

Tangy Meatloaf Burgers

SERVES 4

ACTIVE: 30 min

TOTAL: 30 min

1 small onion (½ sliced into rings, ½ diced)

1 pound meatloaf mix (ground pork, beef and veal) or ground turkey

¼ cup fresh parsley, chopped

½ cup panko breadcrumbs

1 large egg

1 teaspoon sweet or smoked paprika

⅓ cup ketchup

⅓ cup duck sauce

Kosher salt and freshly ground pepper

1 tablespoon extra-virgin olive oil

4 potato buns or other rolls, split

Lettuce, sliced tomato and pickle slices, for topping

Sweet potato chips, for serving (optional)

A ketchup–duck sauce glaze gives these burgers extra flavor. If you don't have duck sauce, use orange marmalade or peach preserves mixed with a splash of water.

1. Preheat a grill to medium high. Soak the onion rings in a bowl of cold water. Meanwhile, combine the ground meat with the diced onion, parsley, breadcrumbs, egg, paprika, 1 tablespoon each ketchup and duck sauce, 1 teaspoon salt and ½ teaspoon pepper. Gently form into four 1-inch-thick patties; make an indentation in the center of each.

2. Brush the patties with the olive oil and grill until marked on the bottom, about 6 minutes. Meanwhile, mix the remaining ketchup and duck sauce in a small bowl for brushing; set aside a few tablespoons for topping. Turn the patties, brush with the ketchup mixture and continue grilling until cooked through, about 5 more minutes. Toast the buns, if desired.

3. Spread the buns with the reserved ketchup mixture. Drain the onion rings. Serve the patties on the buns; top with onion, lettuce, tomato and pickles. Serve with sweet potato chips.

Per serving: Calories 444; Fat 19 g (Saturated 6 g); Cholesterol 123 mg; Sodium 1,079 mg; Carbohydrate 43 g; Fiber 2 g; Protein 26 g

Veggie Burger Pockets
Vegetarian

SERVES 4

ACTIVE: 30 min
TOTAL: 30 min

2 large eggs

4 frozen veggie burgers

½ cup nonfat plain Greek yogurt

1 small clove garlic, finely grated

¼ teaspoon hot paprika

Kosher salt

4 cups baby arugula

½ cup jarred sliced roasted red peppers

1 Kirby cucumber, thinly sliced

1 tablespoon extra-virgin olive oil

1 teaspoon dried mint, crumbled

¼ cup crumbled feta cheese

4 large whole-wheat pitas, warmed

Pickles, for serving (optional)

Turn frozen veggie burgers into this quick, healthful dinner. Look for patties that are low in sodium—brands vary a lot.

1. Place the eggs in a small saucepan and cover with water by about 1 inch. Bring to a rapid simmer over medium-high heat and cook for 1 minute. Cover, remove from the heat and let sit 12 minutes. Drain the eggs and rinse under cold water, then peel and thinly slice.

2. Meanwhile, cook the veggie burgers as the label directs. Whisk the yogurt, garlic, paprika, 2 tablespoons water, and salt to taste in a small bowl. In a large bowl, toss the arugula, roasted red peppers, cucumber, olive oil, mint, feta, and salt to taste.

3. Cut 1 inch off the top of each pita to make an opening; stuff the pita strip inside the pita to reinforce the bottom. Fill each pita with a veggie burger, some arugula salad and a few slices of hard-boiled egg. Drizzle with the yogurt dressing. Serve with pickles.

Per serving: Calories 400; Fat 13 g (Saturated 3 g); Cholesterol 116 mg; Sodium 994 mg; Carbohydrate 46 g; Fiber 6 g; Protein 25 g

Turkey-Avocado Sandwiches

SERVES 4

ACTIVE: 25 min

TOTAL: 25 min

⅓ cup thinly sliced red onion

2 tablespoons apple cider vinegar

8 slices turkey bacon

1 Hass avocado, halved and pitted

½ cup nonfat plain Greek yogurt

Kosher salt and freshly ground pepper

8 slices whole-grain bread, lightly toasted

8 small leaves romaine lettuce

1 tomato, cut into 8 slices

12 ounces deli-sliced low-sodium turkey breast

½ small English cucumber, sliced

Add some good fat to your sandwiches: Instead of mayo, we made a spread of mashed avocado and Greek yogurt.

1. Toss the onion with the vinegar and 2 tablespoons water in a small bowl. Let stand 15 minutes, then drain. Meanwhile, cook the turkey bacon as the label directs until crisp.

2. Mash the avocado with the yogurt in another small bowl until smooth. Season with salt and pepper.

3. Spread the avocado-yogurt mixture on the bread. Top 4 of the slices with the lettuce and tomato and season with salt and pepper. Add the turkey breast, bacon, cucumber and red onion; close with the remaining bread slices, spread-side down. Cut each sandwich in half.

Per serving: Calories 418; Fat 17 g (Saturated 4 g); Cholesterol 67 mg; Sodium 1,349 mg; Carbohydrate 39 g; Fiber 14 g; Protein 31 g

Roast Beef Wraps with Dill Slaw

SERVES 4

ACTIVE: 15 min
TOTAL: 15 min

 3 cups shredded coleslaw mix

 ¼ cup chopped fresh dill

 1 tablespoon white wine
   vinegar

 ¼ teaspoon sugar

 ¼ cup mayonnaise

 2 tablespoons sour cream

 2 tablespoons horseradish,
   drained

   Kosher salt and freshly
   ground pepper

 ¼ pound dill-flavored havarti
   cheese, thinly sliced

 ½ pound deli-sliced roast beef

 4 whole-wheat wraps

   Vegetable or potato chips, for
   serving (optional)

Instead of buying presliced packaged cheese, hit the deli counter and ask someone to custom-slice something new, like havarti, gruyère or chipotle gouda.

1. Make the slaw: Toss the coleslaw mix, dill, vinegar, sugar, mayonnaise, sour cream, horseradish, ¾ teaspoon salt, and pepper to taste in a bowl.

2. Layer the cheese, roast beef and slaw in the center of the wraps. Fold in the sides, then roll up tightly. Cut in half and serve with chips.

Per serving (without chips): Calories 434; Fat 25 g (Saturated 9 g); Cholesterol 71 mg; Sodium 1,061 mg; Carbohydrate 26 g; Fiber 1 g; Protein 25 g

Steak and Hummus Sandwiches

SERVES 4

ACTIVE: 20 min
TOTAL: 20 min

Vegetable oil, for the grill

1 pound flank steak

Kosher salt and freshly ground pepper

½ red onion, thinly sliced

½ cup sliced pickled banana peppers, plus ½ cup juice from the jar

½ cup hummus

2 tablespoons extra-virgin olive oil

4 pocketless pitas (preferably whole wheat)

8 romaine lettuce leaves, thinly sliced

Hot sauce, for topping (optional)

Flank steak (often labeled as London broil) is an inexpensive lean cut, but it can be tough. To keep it tender, cook it to medium rare and then thinly slice it against the grain.

1. Preheat a grill to medium high; brush the grates with vegetable oil. Season the steak with salt and pepper; grill 5 to 6 minutes per side for medium rare. Set aside at least 5 minutes before slicing.

2. Meanwhile, toss the red onion, banana peppers and ⅓ cup of the pickle juice in a bowl. Whisk the hummus with 3 to 4 tablespoons water in another bowl until smooth and pourable.

3. Thinly slice the steak against the grain, then cut crosswise into bite-size pieces. Toss with the remaining pickle juice, 1 tablespoon olive oil, and salt and pepper to taste.

4. Brush the pitas on one side with the remaining 1 tablespoon olive oil and season with salt and pepper. Grill, oiled-side down, until lightly toasted, about 1 minute.

5. Remove the pitas from the grill and top with the steak. Drain the onion and peppers; divide evenly among the pitas. Top with the lettuce and drizzle with the hummus sauce. Top with hot sauce.

Per serving: Calories 480; Fat 19 g (Saturated 5 g); Cholesterol 43 mg; Sodium 461 mg; Carbohydrate 46 g; Fiber 7 g; Protein 32 g

Shrimp and Kale Pitas

SERVES 4

ACTIVE: 25 min
TOTAL: 30 min

½ cup plain low-fat yogurt

3 tablespoons extra-virgin olive oil

Juice of 1 lemon

1 small clove garlic, finely grated

Kosher salt

⅛ teaspoon cayenne pepper

1 small bunch kale, stems removed and leaves thinly sliced

¾ pound medium shrimp, peeled and deveined

1 15-ounce can no-salt-added chickpeas, drained and rinsed

1 pint grape tomatoes, halved

½ small red onion, thinly sliced

4 pieces pita bread, halved

Broiling is a great way to cook shrimp: You don't need much oil, and there's barely any cleanup!

1. Preheat the broiler. Whisk the yogurt, 2½ tablespoons olive oil, the lemon juice, garlic, ¼ teaspoon salt and the cayenne in a large bowl. Add the kale and toss to coat; set aside at room temperature while you prepare the shrimp.

2. Toss the shrimp with the remaining ½ tablespoon olive oil on a foil-lined baking sheet. Broil until just cooked through, 4 to 5 minutes; let cool slightly.

3. Add the shrimp, chickpeas, tomatoes and red onion to the bowl with the kale; toss to coat. Stack the pitas on a plate and warm in the microwave, about 30 seconds. Fill with the shrimp-kale mixture.

Per serving: Calories 554; Fat 15 g (Saturated 2 g); Cholesterol 131 mg; Sodium 669 mg; Carbohydrate 72 g; Fiber 9 g; Protein 35 g

Sardine Salad Sandwiches

SERVES 4

ACTIVE: 15 min

TOTAL: 15 min

- 2 3.75-ounce cans oil-packed skinless, boneless sardines, drained
- 2 stalks celery, finely chopped
- ½ small red onion, finely chopped
- ¼ cup low-fat mayonnaise
- 1 tablespoon chopped fresh dill
- 1 tablespoon fresh lemon juice, plus 1 teaspoon zest
- 1 teaspoon dijon mustard
  Kosher salt and freshly ground pepper
- 8 slices whole-grain bread, toasted
  Bibb lettuce, sliced tomato, sliced cucumber and alfalfa sprouts, for topping

This sandwich is a great way to sneak sardines into your lunch: Sardines are one of the best sources of heart-healthy omega-3 fatty acids, plus they're high in vitamins D and B12.

1. Combine the sardines, celery, red onion, mayonnaise, dill, lemon juice, lemon zest, mustard, ¼ teaspoon salt, and pepper to taste in a large bowl. Mash well with a fork.

2. Sandwich the sardine salad between the bread slices along with the lettuce, tomato, cucumber and sprouts.

Per serving: Calories 294; Fat 13 g (Saturated 2 g); Cholesterol 76 mg; Sodium 785 mg; Carbohydrate 28 g; Fiber 4 g; Protein 18 g

SNACK TIME!

These pretzel snacks are just as addictive as chips—and much better for you.

SMOKY PRETZEL MIX
Melt ½ stick butter with 3 tablespoons brown sugar, 1 teaspoon smoked paprika and ¼ teaspoon cayenne. Toss with 3 cups mini pretzels and 2 cups mixed nuts. Spread on a baking sheet and bake 20 minutes at 325°, stirring.

PRETZEL MELTS
Sandwich small slices of cheddar between mini pretzels. Put on a parchment-lined baking sheet and bake about 10 minutes at 425°. Serve with mustard.

NUTTY PRETZEL WANDS
Spread peanut butter on the top few inches of pretzel rods. Roll in chopped peanuts and/or dried fruit.

CHEESY CHEX MIX
Toss 3 cups Chex cereal, 2 cups mini pretzels and 1 cup cheese crackers with ¾ cup grated parmesan, ½ stick melted butter and a pinch of garlic powder. Spread on a baking sheet and bake 15 minutes at 325°, stirring.

POULTRY

Grilled Chicken Satay Salad

Gluten-Free

SERVES 4

ACTIVE: 25 min

TOTAL: 25 min

2 skinless, boneless chicken
breasts (about 1 pound)

7 tablespoons Thai peanut
sauce

3 tablespoons vegetable oil

Kosher salt and freshly
ground pepper

2 tablespoons fresh lime juice

1 head romaine lettuce, sliced

½ English cucumber or
2 Persian cucumbers, cut
into matchsticks

1 medium carrot, halved
lengthwise and thinly sliced

1 red bell pepper, thinly sliced

¼ cup roughly chopped fresh
cilantro, plus more for
topping

3 tablespoons chopped roasted
salted peanuts

Peanut sauce is a great shortcut ingredient: Keep it on hand
to use as a marinade, a sauce for noodles or a dip for veggies.
If you're cooking gluten-free, check the label: Some brands
contain gluten.

1. Preheat a grill or grill pan to medium high. Slice the chicken breasts into
strips and toss with 2 tablespoons peanut sauce, ½ tablespoon vegetable oil,
¼ teaspoon salt, and pepper to taste in a bowl. Grill the chicken until just
cooked through, about 2 minutes per side. Transfer to a plate.

2. Whisk the remaining 5 tablespoons peanut sauce and 2½ tablespoons
vegetable oil, the lime juice and 2 tablespoons water in a large bowl. Add
the lettuce, cucumber, carrot, bell pepper and cilantro and toss. Season with
salt and pepper and divide among bowls; top with the chicken. Sprinkle
with peanuts and more cilantro.

Per serving: Calories 363; Fat 20 g (Saturated 2 g); Cholesterol 66 mg;
Sodium 208 mg; Carbohydrate 15 g; Fiber 5 g; Protein 32 g

Chicken with Arugula Pesto

SERVES 4

ACTIVE: 35 min
TOTAL: 40 min

Kosher salt

6 ounces orecchiette
(about 1½ cups)

½ pound green beans, trimmed
and cut into pieces

⅓ cup grated parmesan cheese

2 tablespoons extra-virgin
olive oil

1 teaspoon finely grated
lemon zest

3 cups baby arugula

½ cup firmly packed fresh
parsley

2 tablespoons almonds or
hazelnuts, toasted

1 tablespoon fresh lemon juice

4 small skinless, boneless
chicken breasts (about
1¼ pounds)

2 medium tomatoes, halved

2 teaspoons whole-wheat
breadcrumbs

We made this pesto with arugula and parsley instead of basil, but you can swap in other herbs or leafy greens. Try mint, cilantro, watercress or kale, and experiment with different nuts, too.

1. Bring a pot of salted water to a boil. Add the pasta and cook as the label directs; about 3 minutes before the pasta is done, add the green beans and cook until crisp-tender. Drain the pasta and beans and rinse under cold water. Toss with half of the cheese, 1 tablespoon olive oil, the lemon zest and salt.

2. Preheat the broiler. Puree the arugula, parsley, nuts, lemon juice, remaining cheese, 3 tablespoons water, 1 tablespoon olive oil, and salt to taste in a food processor. Transfer to a bowl.

3. Place the chicken breasts between 2 pieces of plastic wrap and pound to about ½ inch thick. Transfer to a foil-lined baking sheet and season with salt. Rub all over with ¼ cup of the arugula pesto and broil until cooked through, 4 to 5 minutes per side.

4. Arrange the tomatoes cut-side up on another baking sheet and broil 2 minutes. Spread with pesto and sprinkle with the breadcrumbs. Broil until golden, 1 more minute. Serve the chicken, tomatoes and pasta salad with the remaining pesto.

Per serving: Calories 491; Fat 16 g (Saturated 4 g); Cholesterol 96 mg; Sodium 737 mg; Carbohydrate 42 g; Fiber 5 g; Protein 44 g

Spicy Chicken Enchiladas
Gluten-Free

SERVES 4

ACTIVE: 30 min
TOTAL: 40 min

- 2 tablespoons extra-virgin olive oil, plus more for brushing
- 1 jalapeño pepper, seeded and sliced
- 3 cloves garlic, smashed
- ½ teaspoon dried thyme or 1½ teaspoons fresh thyme
- 1 white onion, minced
- 8 ounces skinless, boneless chicken breast, halved lengthwise
- Kosher salt
- 1½ pounds tomatoes, cored and roughly chopped
- ½ teaspoon ground allspice
- 8 corn tortillas
- 1½ cups shredded muenster cheese (about 6 ounces)
- 1 cup mixed fresh parsley and cilantro, chopped

This dish is a twist on *entomatadas*, a Mexican enchilada-like dish made with fried tortillas and a spicy tomato sauce. We faked the fried flavor by brushing the tortillas with oil and baking them.

1. Preheat the oven to 450°. Heat 1 tablespoon olive oil in a large skillet over medium-high heat. Add the jalapeño, garlic, thyme and half of the onion. Cook, stirring, until soft, about 3 minutes. Add the chicken, 1 teaspoon salt and ¾ cup water. Bring to a boil, then cover and cook until the chicken is tender, about 6 minutes.

2. Remove the chicken to a plate. Transfer the cooking liquid and vegetables to a blender; add the tomatoes and allspice and puree with the lid slightly ajar. Wipe out the skillet, add the remaining 1 tablespoon olive oil and place over medium-high heat. Add the tomato mixture and cook until slightly reduced, 6 minutes. Pour into a baking dish.

3. Brush the tortillas with olive oil and put on a baking sheet; bake until soft and pliable, 3 to 5 minutes. Shred the chicken. Top each tortilla with chicken and cheese, then roll up and arrange in the baking dish, seam-side down, spooning some of the sauce on top. Bake until the cheese melts, 4 minutes.

4. Toss the herbs, remaining onion, and salt to taste in a bowl. Sprinkle on top of the enchiladas.

Per serving: Calories 452; Fat 23 g (Saturated 9 g); Cholesterol 74 mg; Sodium 852 mg; Carbohydrate 35 g; Fiber 4 g; Protein 27 g

Spiced Couscous and Chicken

SERBES 4

ACTIVE: 30 min

TOTAL: 30 min

¾ teaspoon ground cinnamon

1 teaspoon ground ginger

Kosher salt and freshly ground pepper

4 medium carrots, thinly sliced

1 cup couscous, preferably whole wheat

2 cups coarsely shredded rotisserie chicken

3 tablespoons unsalted butter

½ cup sliced almonds

¼ cup golden raisins

4 scallions (white and light green parts only), roughly chopped

½ cup roughly chopped fresh cilantro, plus more for topping

Greek yogurt and/or harissa or other chile paste, for topping

You can use roast turkey from the deli in place of the chicken in this dish: Just buy a ½-inch-thick slice, then chop it.

1. Bring 2½ cups water to a boil in medium saucepan over medium-high heat. Add ½ teaspoon cinnamon, the ginger, 1 teaspoon salt and ½ teaspoon pepper. Add the carrots and cook until crisp-tender, 3 to 4 minutes. Drain the carrots, reserving the cooking liquid.

2. Put the couscous and chicken in a medium bowl; pour 1 cup of the hot cooking liquid on top. Stir, then cover tightly with plastic wrap and let sit 5 minutes. Fluff the couscous with a fork.

3. Meanwhile, melt the butter in a medium skillet over medium-high heat. Add the almonds, raisins, scallions and the remaining ¼ teaspoon cinnamon. Cook, stirring, until the nuts are toasted, 2 to 3 minutes. Stir in the cilantro.

4. Divide the couscous and chicken among bowls. Top with the carrots and more of the cooking liquid. Sprinkle with the almond mixture. Top with yogurt and/or harissa and more cilantro.

Per serving: Calories 441; Fat 20 g (Saturated 7 g); Cholesterol 91 mg; Sodium 853 mg; Carbohydrate 42 g; Fiber 8 g; Protein 28 g

Chicken Potpie

SERVES 6

ACTIVE: 1 hr
TOTAL: 2 hr

FOR THE CRUST

1 cup all-purpose flour,
  plus more for dusting

¼ teaspoon baking powder

¼ teaspoon fine salt

4 tablespoons cold unsalted
  butter, cut into small pieces

1 large egg

2 tablespoons 2% milk

FOR THE FILLING

2 small russet potatoes

4½ cups low-sodium
  chicken broth

5 carrots, cut into large chunks

1 teaspoon chopped fresh thyme

2 tablespoons extra-virgin
  olive oil

1 large onion, finely diced

3 tablespoons all-purpose flour

⅓ cup 2% milk

3 stalks celery, sliced

3 cups shredded rotisserie
  chicken, skin removed

½ cup fat-free plain Greek yogurt

1 cup frozen peas

½ cup minced fresh parsley

  Kosher salt and freshly
  ground pepper

We cut about 235 calories and 24 grams of fat per serving from the classic potpie! This version calls for Greek yogurt in place of cream.

1. Prepare the crust: Pulse the flour, baking powder and fine salt in a food processor until combined. Add the butter, one piece at a time, pulsing until the mixture looks like coarse meal. Separate the egg; refrigerate the egg white for brushing. Beat the egg yolk and milk in a bowl, then add to the food processor, pulsing until the dough comes together. Turn out onto a lightly floured surface and gather into a ball. Flatten into a disk, wrap in plastic wrap and chill at least 1 hour.

2. Meanwhile, make the filling: Preheat the oven to 425°. Prick the potatoes with a fork and bake directly on the oven rack until tender, about 45 minutes. Let cool slightly, then peel and break into small pieces.

3. Bring the chicken broth, carrots and thyme to a simmer in a small saucepan over medium heat and cook 2 minutes; cover and keep warm. Meanwhile, heat the olive oil in a large pot over medium heat. Add the onion and cook until soft, about 8 minutes. Sprinkle in the flour and stir until lightly toasted, about 3 minutes. Add the milk, celery, potato pieces and the warm broth mixture and simmer until thickened, about 15 minutes. Remove from the heat and stir in the chicken, yogurt, peas and parsley. Season with salt and pepper.

4. Transfer the filling to a 2-quart casserole dish. Roll out the dough on a lightly floured surface until about ⅛ inch thick and slightly larger than the dish. Beat the reserved egg white in a bowl; brush over the dough and season with salt and pepper. Press the dough against the sides of the dish. Place on a baking sheet and bake until the crust is golden brown, 20 to 25 minutes.

Per serving: Calories 482; Fat 19 g (Saturated 8 g); Cholesterol 137 mg; Sodium 795 mg; Carbohydrate 47 g; Fiber 5 g; Protein 31 g

Grilled Chicken with Roasted Kale

Gluten-Free

SERVES 4

ACTIVE: 20 min
TOTAL: 30 min

- ½ pound small red-skinned potatoes, cut into ½-inch pieces
- 2 tablespoons extra-virgin olive oil, plus more for brushing
- 1 large bunch kale, stems removed, leaves torn (about 10 cups)
- 3 cloves garlic, thinly sliced

  Kosher salt and freshly ground pepper
- 2 large skinless, boneless chicken breasts (about 1½ pounds)
- 4 cups mixed salad greens
- ½ cup cherry tomatoes, halved
- ⅓ cup grated parmesan cheese
- 1 tablespoon fresh lemon juice

Roasting kale helps tone down its bitterness, and the greens turn out light and crisp. Eat up: One cup of chopped kale has more vitamin C than a small orange!

1. Preheat the oven to 425°. Toss the potatoes with ½ tablespoon olive oil on a rimmed baking sheet; spread in a single layer and roast 5 minutes. Toss the kale in a large bowl with the garlic, ½ tablespoon olive oil, ¼ teaspoon salt, and pepper to taste. Add to the baking sheet with the potatoes and toss. Roast until the kale is crisp and the potatoes are tender, stirring once, 15 to 20 minutes.

2. Meanwhile, preheat a grill or grill pan to medium and brush with olive oil. Slice the chicken breasts in half horizontally to make 4 cutlets. Coat evenly with ½ tablespoon olive oil and season with salt and pepper. Grill the chicken until well marked and cooked through, 2 to 4 minutes per side. Transfer to a plate.

3. Toss the kale, potatoes, the remaining ½ tablespoon olive oil, the salad greens, tomatoes, parmesan, lemon juice, and salt and pepper to taste in a large bowl. Divide the chicken among plates and top with any collected juices. Serve with the kale salad.

Per serving: Calories 434; Fat 14 g (Saturated 4 g); Cholesterol 112 mg; Sodium 586 mg; Carbohydrate 28 g; Fiber 6 g; Protein 50 g

Chicken with Cacciatore Sauce

Gluten-Free

SERVES 4

ACTIVE: 25 min
TOTAL: 40 min

- 8 skin-on, bone-in chicken thighs (about 2½ pounds)
- Kosher salt and freshly ground pepper
- 3 slices bacon, chopped
- ¼ onion
- 4 ounces cremini mushrooms (about 2 cups)
- 1 teaspoon fresh rosemary
- 1 tablespoon extra-virgin olive oil
- 1 28-ounce can whole San Marzano tomatoes
- ¼ cup dry red wine
- ⅓ cup pitted niçoise or kalamata olives, plus 1 tablespoon brine from the jar

Chefs swear by canned San Marzano tomatoes; they're grown in mineral-rich soil, which gives them great acidity and sweetness. Buy them whole and puree or crush them yourself.

1. Position a rack in the upper third of the oven and preheat to 475°. Pat the chicken dry and season with salt and pepper. Place skin-side up in a shallow baking dish and roast until the skin is golden brown and the chicken is cooked through, about 35 minutes.

2. Meanwhile, pulse the bacon, onion, mushrooms and rosemary in a food processor until finely chopped. Heat the olive oil in a large skillet over medium-high heat. Add the vegetable mixture and ¼ teaspoon salt; cover and cook, stirring occasionally, until softened, about 8 minutes.

3. Puree the tomatoes in the food processor. Add the wine to the skillet and boil, uncovered, until almost completely reduced, 2 to 3 minutes. Add the pureed tomatoes and return to a boil. Reduce the heat, partially cover and simmer, stirring occasionally, until slightly thickened, about 20 minutes. Stir in the olives and brine and season with salt and pepper. Serve the chicken with the sauce.

Per serving: Calories 499; Fat 32 g (Saturated 9 g); Cholesterol 127 mg; Sodium 851 mg; Carbohydrate 11 g; Fiber 2 g; Protein 35 g

Falafel Chicken with Hummus Slaw

SERVES 4

ACTIVE: 25 min
TOTAL: 25 min

Cooking spray

3 skinless, boneless chicken breasts (about 1¼ pounds), sliced into ¼-inch-thick strips

1 tablespoon extra-virgin olive oil

½ cup falafel mix

2 whole-wheat pitas, halved

6 tablespoons hummus

Grated zest and juice of 1 lemon

½ teaspoon harissa or other hot chile paste

4 cups shredded coleslaw mix

6 radishes, halved and thinly sliced

1 cup chopped fresh parsley

Kosher salt

Falafel mix makes a healthful coating for these chicken fingers. Bake the chicken on a wire rack so it will get crisp all around.

1. Preheat the oven to 425°. Set a rack on a rimmed baking sheet and coat with cooking spray. Toss the chicken with the olive oil in a large bowl, then add the falafel mix and toss to coat. Arrange the chicken on the rack and bake until golden and cooked through, about 10 minutes. While the chicken is baking, stack the pita halves and wrap them in foil; warm in the oven, about 5 minutes.

2. Meanwhile, mix the hummus with the lemon zest and juice, harissa and 3 tablespoons water in a large bowl. Remove 2 tablespoons of the hummus sauce and reserve. Add the coleslaw mix, radishes and parsley to the remaining hummus sauce and toss. Season with salt.

3. Divide the chicken among plates and drizzle with the reserved hummus sauce. Stuff the slaw in the pitas and serve with the chicken.

Per serving: Calories 366; Fat 9 g (Saturated 1 g); Cholesterol 82 mg; Sodium 587 mg; Carbohydrate 32 g; Fiber 8 g; Protein 43 g

Chicken Veracruz

Gluten-Free

SERVES 4

ACTIVE: 25 min

TOTAL: 35 min

- 1 tablespoon extra-virgin olive oil
- 4 skin-on, bone-in chicken breasts (about 1½ pounds)
- 1 teaspoon dried oregano
  Kosher salt
- 1 poblano chile pepper, stemmed and seeded
- ½ white onion
- 1 large tomato
- 2 cloves garlic
- ½ cup chopped pickled jalapeño peppers
- ½ cup green olives with pimientos, roughly chopped
- 1 cup dry white wine

This dish is for chile lovers: We used a double dose of peppers, both fresh and pickled.

1. Heat the olive oil in a large deep skillet over high heat. Pat the chicken dry and sprinkle with the oregano and 1 teaspoon salt. Sear the chicken until well browned, about 7 minutes per side.

2. Meanwhile, slice the poblano into strips and thinly slice the onion. Cut the tomato into 8 wedges and smash the garlic.

3. Once the chicken is browned, scatter the poblano, onion, tomato, garlic, jalapeños and olives over and around the chicken. Cook until the vegetables begin softening slightly, about 5 minutes. Sprinkle with ½ teaspoon salt. Add the wine and bring to a boil; cover and simmer until the chicken is cooked through and the vegetables are soft, about 10 minutes. Serve the chicken with the vegetables.

Per serving: Calories 421; Fat 22 g (Saturated 5 g); Cholesterol 109 mg; Sodium 1,304 mg; Carbohydrate 9 g; Fiber 1 g; Protein 36 g

Chicken and Asparagus Crêpes

SERVES 4

ACTIVE: 30 min
TOTAL: 35 min

3 tablespoons unsalted butter, plus more for the dish

2½ cups shredded rotisserie chicken, skin removed

1½ cups ricotta cheese

¾ cup grated parmesan cheese, plus more for serving

¼ cup chopped fresh herbs (such as parsley, dill, chives or mint)

Kosher salt and freshly ground pepper

8 store-bought crêpes (about 9 inches each)

1 shallot, sliced

½ pound asparagus, trimmed and cut into pieces

¾ cup low-sodium chicken broth

1 teaspoon finely grated lemon zest

Look for premade crêpes near the produce section of your supermarket. You can use them for dinner or dessert, and each one is only about 60 calories.

1. Preheat the oven to 425°. Butter a large baking dish. Combine the chicken with the ricotta, ½ cup parmesan, 3 tablespoons herbs, ¾ teaspoon salt and ½ teaspoon pepper in a medium bowl. Spoon about ¼ cup of the chicken mixture across the lower half of each crêpe; roll up to enclose the filling. Place the crêpes, seam-side down, in the baking dish. Cover with foil and bake until the filling is hot, about 15 minutes.

2. Meanwhile, melt 3 tablespoons butter in a skillet over medium-high heat. Add the shallot and cook until it softens, about 1 minute. Add the asparagus and cook until just tender, about 3 minutes. Add the chicken broth, lemon zest and the remaining 1 tablespoon herbs and simmer until the sauce is slightly thickened, about 2 minutes. Stir in the remaining ¼ cup parmesan and season with salt and pepper.

3. Divide the crêpes among plates, top with the asparagus and sauce, and sprinkle with parmesan.

Per serving: Calories 405; Fat 24 g (Saturated 14 g); Cholesterol 115 mg; Sodium 984 mg; Carbohydrate 19 g; Fiber 1 g; Protein 26 g

Spanish Chicken with Potato Roast

Gluten-Free

SERVES 4

ACTIVE: 20 min

TOTAL: 40 min

- 1½ pounds large Yukon gold potatoes, cut into 1½-inch pieces
- 4 cloves garlic, smashed and coarsely chopped
- 2 tablespoons extra-virgin olive oil

  Kosher salt
- 1½ pounds skinless, boneless chicken thighs (5 to 6 thighs)
- 2 teaspoons smoked paprika

  Freshly ground pepper
- 4 tablespoons roughly chopped fresh parsley
- 2 lemons (1 juiced, 1 cut into wedges)
- 2 large or 3 medium red onions, halved and thinly sliced

When you're roasting potatoes, preheat the baking dish or sheet in the oven. The potatoes will end up with a nice brown crust.

1. Position a rack in the upper third of the oven. Place a large cast-iron baking dish or a rimmed baking sheet on the rack; preheat to 500°. Put the potatoes, garlic, olive oil, 1 tablespoon water and ½ teaspoon salt in a large microwave-safe baking dish and toss to coat. Cover with plastic wrap, pierce the plastic in a few places with a knife and microwave 8 minutes to partially cook.

2. Meanwhile, pat the chicken dry and transfer to a bowl. Sprinkle with the paprika, 1 teaspoon salt and ½ teaspoon pepper. Add 2 tablespoons parsley and the lemon juice; toss to coat. Set aside.

3. Remove the hot baking dish from the oven; carefully add the potatoes and spread in an even layer. Scatter the onions on top. Roast until the potatoes start browning, about 12 minutes.

4. Flip the potatoes and lay the chicken pieces on top, adding any accumulated juices from the bowl; return to the oven and roast until the potatoes are tender and the chicken is cooked through, about 12 more minutes. Remove from the oven and top with the remaining 2 tablespoons parsley. Serve with the lemon wedges.

Per serving: Calories 452; Fat 14 g (Saturated 3 g); Cholesterol 141 mg; Sodium 882 mg; Carbohydrate 41 g; Fiber 4 g; Protein 39 g

Chicken Salad with Gazpacho Dressing

SERVES 4

ACTIVE: 30 min
TOTAL: 30 min

Cooking spray

1 pound chicken cutlets

Kosher salt and freshly ground pepper

4 slices crusty bread

1 clove garlic, halved

2 tablespoons extra-virgin olive oil

1 tablespoon sherry vinegar or red wine vinegar

½ English cucumber, diced

1 cup cherry tomatoes, quartered

1 cup fresh parsley

⅓ cup sliced almonds, toasted

8 cups baby arugula (about 8 ounces)

1 15-ounce can chickpeas, drained and rinsed

Make a big batch of toasted almonds to use in salads: Spread the nuts on a baking sheet and bake at 350°, stirring once or twice, until golden and fragrant, about 10 minutes. Let cool, then transfer to a resealable plastic bag and store in the freezer.

1. Preheat a grill pan over medium heat and lightly coat with cooking spray. Sprinkle the chicken with ¼ teaspoon each salt and pepper. Grill until well marked and cooked through, 3 to 5 minutes per side; transfer to a plate. Add the bread to the pan and grill until toasted, 2 to 3 minutes per side. Transfer to a plate and rub with the garlic.

2. Make the dressing: Puree the olive oil, vinegar, 2 tablespoons water, half each of the cucumber, tomatoes, parsley and almonds, ½ teaspoon salt, and pepper to taste in a blender until smooth.

3. Cut the chicken into strips. Tear the bread into bite-size pieces. Combine the arugula, chickpeas, chicken, bread and the remaining cucumber, tomatoes, parsley and almonds in a large bowl. Add half of the dressing, season with salt and pepper and toss. Divide among bowls. Drizzle with the remaining dressing.

Per serving: Calories 437; Fat 15 g (Saturated 2 g); Cholesterol 63 mg; Sodium 661 mg; Carbohydrate 39 g; Fiber 7 g; Protein 35 g

Honey-Mustard Chicken and Apples

SERVES 4

ACTIVE: 30 min

TOTAL: 40 min

- 8 skin-on, bone-in chicken thighs (2 to 2½ pounds)
- Kosher salt and freshly ground pepper
- 2 tablespoons extra-virgin olive oil
- 1 large onion, cut into large chunks
- 2 cooking apples (such as Cortland), cut into chunks
- 1 cup low-sodium chicken broth
- 3 tablespoons honey mustard
- 1½ teaspoons unsalted butter, softened
- 1 tablespoon all-purpose flour
- Chopped fresh parsley, for topping

This recipe is extra forgiving: Chicken thighs have more fat than breasts, so they won't dry out as easily in the oven.

1. Preheat the oven to 450˚. Season the chicken with salt and pepper. Heat the olive oil in a large ovenproof skillet over medium-high heat. Working in batches if necessary, add the chicken, skin-side down, and cook until golden, about 6 minutes. Flip and cook 2 to 3 more minutes, then transfer to a plate. Pour off all but 2 tablespoons of the drippings.

2. Add the onion and apples to the skillet and season with salt and pepper. Cook until slightly softened, about 4 minutes. Mix the broth with the mustard, then add to the skillet and bring to a boil. Arrange the chicken, skin-side up, in the skillet. Transfer to the oven and roast until the chicken is cooked through, 15 to 20 minutes.

3. Mix the butter and flour to form a paste. Use a slotted spoon to transfer the chicken, apples and onion to plates. Bring the pan juices to a simmer, whisk in about half of the butter-flour mixture and boil to thicken, 2 minutes. Continue to cook, adding more of the butter-flour mixture as needed to make a slightly thick gravy. Season with salt and pepper. Pour over the chicken and sprinkle with the parsley.

Per serving: Calories 457; Fat 28 g (Saturated 7 g); Cholesterol 122 mg; Sodium 200 mg; Carbohydrate 18 g; Fiber 2 g; Protein 33 g

Turkey Cutlets with Plum Salad

Gluten-Free

SERVES 4

ACTIVE: 35 min

TOTAL: 35 min

1½ pounds turkey cutlets

Pinch of cayenne pepper

1¼ teaspoons ground coriander

Kosher salt and freshly ground black pepper

5 tablespoons extra-virgin olive oil

3 firm plums, cut into 1-inch wedges

2 teaspoons fresh lemon juice

8 cups baby arugula (about 8 ounces)

Grilled fruit is the perfect low-fat side dish: Brush plum or peach wedges or sliced pineapple with oil and grill until marked. The sugars in the fruit will caramelize over the flame.

1. Preheat a grill to medium high. One at a time, place the turkey cutlets between 2 sheets of plastic wrap and pound with a meat mallet or heavy skillet until ¼ inch thick. Transfer the cutlets to a bowl and toss with the cayenne, 1 teaspoon coriander, 1 teaspoon salt, ¼ teaspoon black pepper and 1 tablespoon olive oil. Set aside.

2. Toss the plums with the remaining ¼ teaspoon coriander, a pinch of salt and 1 tablespoon olive oil. Grill the plums, turning once, until just starting to soften, 3 to 4 minutes. Set aside.

3. Grill the turkey until cooked through, about 2 minutes per side.

4. Finely chop a few of the grilled plum wedges; put in a large bowl. Stir in the lemon juice, the remaining 3 tablespoons olive oil and ¼ teaspoon each salt and black pepper. Add the arugula and toss. Top the turkey with the salad and the remaining grilled plums.

Per serving: Calories 371; Fat 19 g (Saturated 2 g); Cholesterol 68 mg; Sodium 641 mg; Carbohydrate 7 g; Fiber 1 g; Protein 43 g

Spicy Turkey Lettuce Cups

SERVES 4

ACTIVE: 35 min
TOTAL: 35 min

- 4 ounces thin rice noodles
- 2 tablespoons roasted peanut oil or vegetable oil
- Juice of 3 limes, plus wedges for serving
- 4 teaspoons teriyaki sauce
- 1 small red or green jalapeño pepper (remove seeds for less heat)
- 1 2-inch piece ginger, peeled
- Finely grated zest of 1 lime
- 1 medium onion, thinly sliced
- 2 medium bell peppers (1 red, 1 yellow), thinly sliced
- 1 pound ground turkey
- ¼ cup roasted unsalted cashews, roughly chopped
- ½ cup roughly chopped fresh cilantro and/or mint
- 2 romaine lettuce hearts, leaves separated

Lettuce cups are a fun way to serve dinner. Use romaine, Bibb or Boston lettuce leaves—they're malleable but sturdy.

1. Cook the noodles as the label directs, then drain and toss with 1 tablespoon roasted peanut oil. Meanwhile, whisk the lime juice and 2 teaspoons teriyaki sauce in a small bowl. Combine the jalapeño, ginger and lime zest in a mini food processor and pulse until finely chopped, or finely chop with a knife.

2. Heat the remaining 1 tablespoon roasted peanut oil in a large nonstick skillet over medium-high heat. Add the onion and cook, stirring, until soft, 5 minutes. Add the ginger mixture and cook, stirring, until toasted, 1 minute. Add the bell peppers and cook, stirring, 3 more minutes. Add the turkey and the remaining 2 teaspoons teriyaki sauce; cook, stirring, until the meat is cooked through, about 5 more minutes.

3. Remove from the heat and stir in the lime juice mixture, cashews and herbs. Pile the noodles and turkey mixture in the lettuce leaves. Serve with lime wedges.

Per serving: Calories 410; Fat 18 g (Saturated 4 g); Cholesterol 65 mg; Sodium 191 mg; Carbohydrate 37 g; Fiber 3 g; Protein 26 g

Turkey and Green Bean Stir-Fry

SERVES 4

ACTIVE: 30 min
TOTAL: 30 min

- 1½ cups basmati rice
- 1½ pounds green beans, trimmed
- 3 tablespoons vegetable oil
- ½ teaspoon sugar
- ¾ pound 99% lean ground turkey
- 1 clove garlic, minced
- 1 small half-sour pickle, finely chopped
- 2 teaspoons Asian chile paste, such as sambal oelek
- 1 cup low-sodium chicken broth
- 2 tablespoons low-sodium soy sauce
- 1 tablespoon dry sherry or rice vinegar (not seasoned)
- 2 teaspoons cornstarch

Try cooking green beans under the broiler for a change: It gives them a slightly charred flavor and a little crunch.

1. Bring a large pot of water to a boil. Stir in the rice, cover and boil until tender, about 18 minutes; drain well and keep warm.

2. Meanwhile, preheat the broiler. Toss the green beans, 1½ tablespoons vegetable oil and the sugar on a rimmed baking sheet. Broil, stirring once, until the beans are tender and charred, about 8 minutes.

3. Heat the remaining 1½ tablespoons vegetable oil in a large skillet over high heat. Add the turkey and cook, breaking it up with a wooden spoon, until browned, 3 minutes. Add the garlic, pickle and chile paste and cook until the garlic is slightly golden, about 3 minutes.

4. Whisk the chicken broth, soy sauce, sherry and cornstarch in a bowl. Add the green beans to the skillet with the turkey mixture and cook, stirring, 1 minute. Add the soy sauce mixture and cook, stirring occasionally, until the sauce thickens slightly, about 3 minutes. Serve with the rice.

Per serving: Calories 480; Fat 13 g (Saturated 1 g); Cholesterol 40 mg; Sodium 506 mg; Carbohydrate 65 g; Fiber 7 g; Protein 30 g

SNACK TIME!

Try a fresh take on your favorite Mexican dips.

MARGARITA GUACAMOLE

Mash 3 avocados; stir in ¼ cup chopped scallions, ½ cup each diced plum tomato and chopped cilantro, and 1 diced seeded jalapeño. Add the zest and juice of 1 lime, the juice of ½ orange and 3 tablespoons tequila; season with salt. Serve in a salt-rimmed bowl with lime wedges.

MANGO-HABANERO SALSA

Toss 2 diced tomatoes, 1 diced mango, ¼ cup diced red onion, 1 minced seeded habanero chile, 1 minced garlic clove, ⅓ cup chopped cilantro and the juice of 1 to 2 limes. Season with salt.

CHERRY TOMATO SALSA
Toss 1 pint quartered cherry tomatoes, 1 chopped seeded jalapeño, ¼ cup chopped red onion, 2 tablespoons each chopped cilantro and parsley, the juice of 1 lime, and salt to taste.

CORN-BACON GUACAMOLE
Grill 2 ears of corn until charred; cut off the kernels. Mash 3 avocados; stir in ¼ cup diced white onion and ½ cup each diced plum tomato and chopped cilantro. Add the corn, 6 slices crumbled cooked bacon and ⅓ cup chopped pickled jalapeños. Add lime juice and salt to taste.

MEAT

Steak Salad with Roasted Celery

Gluten-Free

SERVES 4

ACTIVE: 35 min

TOTAL: 40 min

- 10 stalks celery (about 1 bunch), cut into 1-inch pieces
- 4 teaspoons extra-virgin olive oil

  Kosher salt and freshly ground pepper
- 2 tablespoons light mayonnaise

  Juice of 2 limes
- 2 tablespoons honey
- 1 tablespoon green hot sauce
- 1 small head iceberg lettuce, shredded
- 1 bunch watercress, torn (3 to 4 cups)
- 1¼ pounds blade steak, about ¾ inch thick (4 to 6 steaks)
- 2 bunches scallions, cut into 2-inch pieces
- 1 cup grape or cherry tomatoes, halved

Top blade steak is a lean, inexpensive cut that comes from the shoulder. Before serving, make sure to remove the tough membrane that runs through the middle.

1. Preheat the oven to 450°. Toss the celery, 1 teaspoon olive oil, and salt and pepper to taste on a foil-lined rimmed baking sheet; roast until tender, about 20 minutes.

2. Whisk the mayonnaise, 2 teaspoons olive oil, the lime juice, honey, hot sauce and 1 tablespoon water in a large bowl. Add the roasted celery and toss. Add the lettuce and watercress but don't toss.

3. Heat a large grill pan or cast-iron skillet over high heat. Rub the steak with the remaining 1 teaspoon olive oil and season with salt and pepper. When the pan is very hot, add the steak and cook, undisturbed, about 3 to 4 minutes per side for medium rare. Transfer to a cutting board. Add the scallions to the pan and cook until charred, about 2 minutes per side.

4. Slice the steak against the grain, discarding the tough membrane that runs through the center. Add the steak and tomatoes to the bowl with the salad and toss to coat. Divide among plates.

Per serving: Calories 418; Fat 22 g (Saturated 7 g); Cholesterol 96 mg; Sodium 413 mg; Carbohydrate 25 g; Fiber 6 g; Protein 31 g

Grilled Steak with Barley Salad

SERVES 4

ACTIVE: 40 min

TOTAL: 40 min

1 1¼-to-1½-pound boneless
sirloin steak

Kosher salt and freshly
ground pepper

1 tablespoon Worcestershire
sauce

3 tablespoons extra-virgin
olive oil

1 cup quick-cooking barley

2 small carrots, sliced

2 stalks celery, halved
lengthwise and sliced

2 cups baby spinach

3 ounces button mushrooms,
stems removed, caps thinly
sliced (about 1 cup)

4 scallions, thinly sliced

2 teaspoons whole-grain
or dijon mustard

1 teaspoon finely grated
lemon zest, plus the juice
of 1 lemon

To check a steak for doneness, insert a thermometer into the side, not the top, and aim the tip of the thermometer toward the center of the meat for the most accurate reading.

1. Preheat a grill to high. Pierce the steak in a few spots with a fork and season with salt and pepper. Mix the Worcestershire sauce and 1 tablespoon olive oil in a large bowl; add the steak and turn to coat. Grill the steak until marked on both sides and a thermometer inserted sideways into the center registers 125°, about 7 minutes per side. Transfer to a cutting board and let rest 5 to 10 minutes.

2. Meanwhile, cook the barley as the label directs. Remove from the heat and stir in the carrots, celery, spinach, mushrooms and scallions; cover to wilt the spinach.

3. Whisk the mustard, lemon zest and juice and the remaining 2 tablespoons olive oil in a bowl. Add the barley mixture to the bowl and toss. Season with salt and pepper.

4. Thinly slice the steak against the grain and season with salt and pepper. Divide among plates and serve with the barley salad.

Per serving: Calories 436; Fat 17 g (Saturated 4 g); Cholesterol 58 mg; Sodium 358 mg; Carbohydrate 37 g; Fiber 6 g; Protein 36 g

Sweet-and-Spicy Mini Meatloaves

SERVES 4

ACTIVE: 25 min
TOTAL: 35 min

- 2 slices whole-grain sandwich bread, torn into pieces
- ½ small onion, quartered
- 1 medium carrot, quartered
- ½ pound 93% lean ground turkey
- ½ pound 90% lean ground beef
- 1 large egg
- ½ teaspoon plus ⅛ teaspoon curry powder
- Kosher salt and freshly ground pepper
- 1 tablespoon ketchup
- 1 tablespoon peach chutney or apricot jam
- 2 medium red-skinned potatoes, sliced ¼ inch thick
- 1 head broccoli (florets cut into pieces, stem peeled and thinly sliced)
- 1 tablespoon extra-virgin olive oil

To lighten up meatloaf, meatballs or other ground-meat dishes, combine equal parts ground beef or pork with a leaner meat like turkey or chicken. If you go all poultry, you'll lose that beefy taste.

1. Preheat the oven to 375°. Pulse the bread in a food processor until finely ground; transfer to a large bowl. Add the onion and carrot to the food processor and pulse until finely chopped. Transfer to the bowl with the bread and add the turkey, beef, egg and ½ teaspoon each curry powder, salt and pepper. Mix by hand until just combined. Shape into 4 small oblong meatloaves on a foil-lined rimmed baking sheet.

2. Mix the ketchup and chutney in a small bowl and brush over the meatloaves. Transfer to the oven and bake until just cooked through, about 20 minutes.

3. Meanwhile, bring a pot of salted water to a boil. Add the potatoes and cook 4 minutes, then add the broccoli florets and stem; cook until the vegetables are just tender, about 6 more minutes. Drain and return to the pot. Toss with the olive oil and the remaining ⅛ teaspoon curry powder. Season with salt and pepper. Serve with the meatloaves.

Per serving: Calories 367; Fat 15 g (Saturated 4 g); Cholesterol 123 mg; Sodium 459 mg; Carbohydrate 32 g; Fiber 7 g; Protein 29 g

Sirloin with Teriyaki Broth

SERVES 4

ACTIVE: 25 min

TOTAL: 25 min

- 1 bunch radishes (with greens)
- 5 tablespoons teriyaki sauce
- 3 tablespoons oyster sauce
- 3 teaspoons grated peeled ginger

  Freshly ground pepper
- 1½ pounds boneless sirloin steak (about 1½ inches thick)

  Vegetable oil, for the pan
- 2 tablespoons rice vinegar (not seasoned)
- 1 tablespoon packed brown sugar
- 2 small sweet potatoes, peeled and sliced ¼ inch thick
- 1 bunch scallions (white and green parts separated), cut into 1½-inch pieces

  Toasted sesame oil, for drizzling

Toasted sesame oil has a relatively low smoke point, so it's not ideal for grilling or searing meat. Use it as a finishing oil instead—it adds a great nutty flavor.

1. Roughly chop the radish greens. Cut the radishes into eighths.

2. Heat a grill pan over medium-high heat. Mix 2 tablespoons teriyaki sauce, 2 tablespoons oyster sauce, 1 teaspoon ginger and ½ teaspoon pepper in a bowl, then spread over the steak. Brush the grill pan with vegetable oil, then cook the steak about 5 minutes per side for medium rare. Transfer to a cutting board and let rest 5 minutes, then thinly slice.

3. Meanwhile, bring the remaining 3 tablespoons teriyaki sauce, 1 tablespoon oyster sauce and 2 teaspoons ginger, the vinegar, brown sugar and 2½ cups water to a simmer in a saucepan, stirring to dissolve the sugar. Add the sweet potatoes, radish wedges and scallion whites, cover and cook, stirring occasionally, until just tender, about 10 minutes. Add the radish and scallion greens and cook until crisp-tender, about 5 minutes. Divide the vegetables, broth and steak among shallow bowls. Drizzle with sesame oil.

Per serving: Calories 336; Fat 9 g (Saturated 3 g); Cholesterol 69 mg; Sodium 403 mg; Carbohydrate 24 g; Fiber 3 g; Protein 38 g

Chile-Rubbed Steak with Creamed Corn
Gluten-Free

SERVES 4

ACTIVE: 30 min

TOTAL: 40 min

- 1 tablespoon ancho chile powder
- 2 teaspoons sugar
- Kosher salt and freshly ground pepper
- 1½ pounds flank steak
- 2 tablespoons extra-virgin olive oil
- 1 white onion, diced
- 2 Cubanelle or banana peppers (or 1 large green bell pepper), seeded and diced
- 2 cups frozen corn
- 1 5-ounce can evaporated milk (about ⅔ cup)
- 3 scallions, thinly sliced
- Lime wedges, for serving

The secret to this light creamed corn is evaporated milk: It adds richness without all the fat and calories of heavy cream.

1. Preheat the broiler. Combine the chile powder, sugar and 1 teaspoon each salt and pepper in a small bowl. Brush the steak all over with 1 tablespoon olive oil, then rub the spice blend on both sides. Transfer to a broiler pan; let sit 10 minutes.

2. Meanwhile, heat the remaining 1 tablespoon olive oil in a medium saucepan over medium-high heat. Add the onion and peppers and cook, stirring occasionally, until the onion is translucent, about 4 minutes. Add the frozen corn; cook, stirring, 2 minutes. Reduce the heat to medium and add the evaporated milk. Cook until thick and creamy, about 7 minutes. Season with salt and pepper.

3. Broil the steak 3 to 4 minutes per side for medium rare. Transfer to a cutting board and let rest 5 to 10 minutes, then thinly slice against the grain. Serve the steak with the creamed corn; sprinkle with the scallions and serve with lime wedges.

Per serving: Calories 452; Fat 22 g (Saturated 8 g); Cholesterol 76 mg; Sodium 633 mg; Carbohydrate 23 g; Fiber 4 g; Protein 40 g

Lamb Steak with Olive Salsa

Gluten-Free

SERVES 4

ACTIVE: 35 min

TOTAL: 35 min

- 2 tablespoons extra-virgin olive oil
- 3 cloves garlic, chopped
- 4 sprigs rosemary, leaves stripped
- 1¼ pounds boneless lamb steak

  Kosher salt and freshly ground pepper
- ⅓ cup chopped fresh parsley
- ¾ cup pitted green Spanish olives, coarsely chopped
- 3 lemons, halved
- 4 to 6 banana or Cubanelle peppers, halved lengthwise and seeded
- 2 bunches scallions

Lamb steak is a lean cut that's great for grilling. If you can't find it, ask a butcher to cut a piece from the leg. You can also make this recipe with skirt steak.

1. Preheat a grill to high. Combine the olive oil, garlic and rosemary in a shallow dish. Add the lamb, turn to coat and season with salt and pepper. Mix the parsley and olives in a bowl.

2. Squeeze the juice of 1 lemon into a bowl. Put the peppers skin-side down on the grill; cook until blistered, brushing with the lemon juice and seasoning with salt, about 4 minutes per side. Transfer to a platter.

3. Meanwhile, grill the remaining 2 lemons cut-side down until charred, about 5 minutes; set aside. Grill the scallions, turning, until tender, about 4 minutes. Transfer to a cutting board and coarsely chop, then add to the olive mixture and season with salt and pepper.

4. Grill the lamb until marked, about 4 minutes per side for medium rare. (A thermometer inserted into the thickest part should register 140°.) Transfer to a cutting board and let rest 5 minutes. Slice against the grain, add to the platter and top with the scallion-olive mixture. Squeeze the grilled lemons on top.

Per serving: Calories 346; Fat 19 g (Saturated 5 g); Cholesterol 95 mg; Sodium 313 mg; Carbohydrate 12 g; Fiber 4 g; Protein 31 g

Pork Tenderloin with Red Cabbage Slaw

SERVES 4

ACTIVE: 30 min

TOTAL: 40 min

- 4 tablespoons unsalted butter
- ½ small head red cabbage, cored and thinly sliced
- ⅓ cup golden raisins
- 3 tablespoons red wine vinegar, plus more to taste
- 1 cup apple cider
- ½ teaspoon ground allspice
- Kosher salt and freshly ground pepper
- 2 small pork tenderloins (1¾ pounds total), halved crosswise
- 1 tablespoon extra-virgin olive oil
- 1½ cups low-sodium chicken broth
- 1 teaspoon all-purpose flour
- 2 tablespoons horseradish, drained

To give meat a nice golden crust, heat your skillet for 30 seconds before you add the oil. This lets the pan get screaming hot without overheating the oil.

1. Preheat the oven to 400°. Melt 3 tablespoons butter in a pot over medium-high heat. Add the cabbage, raisins, vinegar, cider, ¼ teaspoon allspice and ½ teaspoon each salt and pepper; bring to a boil. Reduce the heat and simmer, covered, 20 minutes. Uncover and simmer until the liquid is almost completely absorbed. Season with salt and add more vinegar to taste.

2. Meanwhile, sprinkle the pork with the remaining ¼ teaspoon allspice, 1¼ teaspoons salt and ½ teaspoon pepper. Heat an ovenproof skillet over medium-high heat, then add the olive oil. Add the pork and cook until browned on all sides, then transfer to a roasting pan (reserve the skillet) and roast until a thermometer inserted into the meat registers 145° to 150°, 10 to 15 minutes. Transfer to a cutting board.

3. Boil the broth in the skillet until reduced by one-third. Mix the flour and the remaining 1 tablespoon butter, whisk into the broth and boil 1 minute. Stir in the horseradish. Slice the pork; serve with the cabbage and sauce.

Per serving: Calories 496; Fat 22 g (Saturated 10 g); Cholesterol 168 mg; Sodium 208 mg; Carbohydrate 28 g; Fiber 4 g; Protein 46 g

Roasted Pork with Lentils and Squash

SERVES 4

ACTIVE: 35 min

TOTAL: 40 min

- ¾ cup dried French green lentils
- ¾ pound cubed peeled butternut squash (½ medium squash)
- 2 bay leaves
- 2 tablespoons dijon mustard
- 6 sprigs thyme, leaves stripped
- 1 large pork tenderloin (about 1¼ pounds)
- 2 tablespoons panko breadcrumbs
- 2 slices bacon, chopped
- 4 shallots, thinly sliced
- 1 stalk celery, diced
- ½ cup dry red wine
- ½ cup finely chopped fresh parsley

To break down butternut squash, cut off both ends and scoop the seeds out of the wide end with a spoon, then remove the skin with a vegetable peeler.

1. Preheat the oven to 450°. Combine the lentils, squash, bay leaves and 2½ cups water in a saucepan. Bring to a boil, then reduce the heat to medium low, cover and cook until tender, about 25 minutes. Discard the bay leaves.

2. Meanwhile, mix the mustard and thyme in a small bowl; brush all over the pork. Place the pork on a baking sheet and sprinkle with the breadcrumbs. Transfer to the oven and roast until a thermometer inserted into the thickest part registers 145°, 20 to 25 minutes.

3. Meanwhile, combine the bacon, shallots and celery in a medium skillet and cook over medium heat, stirring occasionally, until the bacon is crisp and the shallots are golden, about 8 minutes. Add the wine and cook until it evaporates, about 5 more minutes. Stir in the parsley.

4. Remove the pork from the oven, cover loosely with foil and let rest 5 minutes, then slice. Serve with the lentils and squash. Spoon the bacon mixture on top.

Per serving: Calories 454; Fat 11 g (Saturated 3 g); Cholesterol 100 mg; Sodium 384 mg; Carbohydrate 41 g; Fiber 7 g; Protein 44 g

Sweet and Sour Pork Stir-Fry

SERVES 4

ACTIVE: 25 min
TOTAL: 25 min

  1 pork tenderloin (about 1 pound),
     cut into ½-inch pieces

2½ tablespoons balsamic vinegar
     Kosher salt

  2 teaspoons low-sodium
     soy sauce

  1 tablespoon cornstarch

  3 tablespoons ketchup

  3 tablespoons sugar,
     plus a pinch

  3 tablespoons peanut
     or vegetable oil

  3 cloves garlic, minced

  2 carrots, thinly sliced

  3 scallions, cut into ½-inch
     pieces

  3 cups snow peas, trimmed
     and cut in half

Balsamic vinegar, ketchup and soy sauce make a tasty instant sweet-and-sour sauce for this recipe. Try it in other stir-fries.

1. Toss the pork with ½ tablespoon vinegar and a pinch of salt in a bowl. Mix the remaining 2 tablespoons vinegar, the soy sauce, cornstarch, ketchup, 3 tablespoons sugar, ⅓ cup water and ½ teaspoon salt in another bowl.

2. Heat 2 tablespoons peanut oil in a large skillet or wok over high heat. Add the pork and slowly stir until it turns mostly opaque, about 2 minutes. Remove the pork with a slotted spoon and transfer to a plate. Discard the oil and wipe out the skillet.

3. Heat the remaining 1 tablespoon peanut oil in the skillet, then stir-fry the garlic with a pinch each of salt and sugar, 15 seconds. Add the carrots and scallions and stir-fry until crisp-tender, 2 minutes. (Add a little water if the garlic starts to stick to the skillet.) Add the pork, snow peas and soy sauce mixture; stir until the pork is cooked through and the sauce is thickened, about 3 minutes.

Per serving: Calories 348; Fat 15 g (Saturated 3 g); Cholesterol 74 mg; Sodium 674 mg; Carbohydrate 27 g; Fiber 4 g; Protein 28 g

Cold Asian Noodle Salad with Pork

SERVES 4

ACTIVE: 30 min
TOTAL: 35 min

2 medium carrots, halved lengthwise and thinly sliced

3 Kirby cucumbers, halved lengthwise and thinly sliced

½ jalapeño pepper, seeded and thinly sliced

⅓ cup rice vinegar (not seasoned)

1 tablespoon fish sauce

Kosher salt and freshly ground pepper

4 ounces rice vermicelli noodles

1½ pounds boneless center-cut pork chops, trimmed of excess fat

3 tablespoons vegetable oil

1 tablespoon hoisin sauce, plus more for brushing

2 cups shredded romaine lettuce

1½ cups fresh cilantro, basil and/or mint

Homemade pickles are a fun way to customize salads and sandwiches, and they don't have to take days. In this recipe we soaked sliced vegetables in a vinegar-based brine for just 20 minutes.

1. Make the pickled vegetables: Put the carrots, cucumbers and jalapeño in a bowl. Heat the rice vinegar and fish sauce in a saucepan, then pour over the vegetables. Add a pinch each of salt and pepper and set aside, stirring occasionally, while you prepare the noodles and pork.

2. Bring a small pot of water to a boil; remove from the heat, add the noodles and let stand 8 minutes. Drain the noodles and rinse under cold water, then snip into smaller pieces with kitchen shears.

3. Meanwhile, season the pork lightly with salt and pepper. Heat 1 tablespoon vegetable oil in a medium skillet over medium-high heat. Add the pork and cook until just cooked through, 3 to 4 minutes per side. Brush each chop with hoisin sauce; flip and cook 30 seconds. Brush with more hoisin sauce, flip and cook 30 more seconds. Remove to a cutting board and let rest 5 minutes, then thinly slice.

4. Divide the noodles among bowls. Strain the pickled vegetables, reserving the liquid. Stir 1 tablespoon hoisin sauce and the remaining 2 tablespoons vegetable oil into the reserved liquid; drizzle over the noodles. Top with the pork, pickled vegetables, lettuce and herbs.

Per serving: Calories 476; Fat 20 g (Saturated 4 g); Cholesterol 78 mg; Sodium 618 mg; Carbohydrate 38 g; Fiber 4 g; Protein 36 g

Roasted Pork with Cajun Slaw

Gluten-Free

SERVES 4

ACTIVE: 25 min

TOTAL: 35 min

- 1 tablespoon plus 2 teaspoons Cajun seasoning
- 1 tablespoon plus 2 teaspoons packed light brown sugar
- 1 large pork tenderloin (about 1½ pounds)
- Kosher salt
- 2 teaspoons extra-virgin olive oil
- ½ cup mayonnaise
- 2 tablespoons Creole or whole-grain mustard
- Juice of 1 lemon
- 2 tablespoons horseradish, drained
- 1 12-ounce package broccoli slaw mix
- 2 small bell peppers (1 red, 1 orange), thinly sliced
- 3 scallions, thinly sliced

We made a quick rub for meat by combining brown sugar with a spice blend. The sugar gives the meat a great caramelized crust, and the spice adds a kick.

1. Preheat the oven to 400°. Mix 1 tablespoon each Cajun seasoning and brown sugar in a small bowl. Sprinkle the pork with ½ teaspoon salt and rub with the sugar-spice mixture. Heat the olive oil in a large ovenproof skillet over medium heat. Add the pork and sear until browned on all sides, about 5 minutes. Transfer to the oven and roast until a thermometer inserted into the thickest part registers 145°, about 18 minutes. Transfer the pork to a cutting board and let rest 5 minutes before slicing.

2. Meanwhile, make the slaw: Whisk the mayonnaise, mustard, lemon juice, horseradish and the remaining 2 teaspoons each Cajun seasoning and brown sugar in a small bowl. Toss the slaw mix, bell peppers and scallions in a large bowl. Add the mayonnaise dressing and toss to coat.

3. Slice the pork and divide among plates. Drizzle with any juices from the skillet. Serve with the slaw.

Per serving: Calories 498; Fat 31 g (Saturated 5 g); Cholesterol 105 mg; Sodium 1,403 mg; Carbohydrate 18 g; Fiber 5 g; Protein 39 g

Pork and Egg Lo Mein

SERVES 4

ACTIVE: 30 min
TOTAL: 35 min

Kosher salt

6 ounces dried lo mein noodles, spaghetti or linguine

3 tablespoons soy sauce

2 tablespoons oyster sauce

2 1-inch-thick boneless pork chops (about ¾ pound), thinly sliced

2½ tablespoons vegetable oil

2 large eggs, lightly beaten

1 bunch scallions, thinly sliced

1 tablespoon finely chopped peeled ginger

2 cloves garlic, finely chopped

4 cups broccoli slaw mix

1 red bell pepper, thinly sliced

To make raw meat easier to slice, freeze it for about 10 minutes until it's just slightly firm.

1. Bring a pot of lightly salted water to a boil. Add the noodles and cook as the label directs. Reserve 3 tablespoons of the cooking water, then drain the noodles and rinse under cold water. Meanwhile, mix the soy sauce and oyster sauce in a small bowl. Put the pork in another bowl and toss with 1 tablespoon of the soy sauce mixture.

2. Heat ½ tablespoon vegetable oil in a large skillet over medium-high heat. Add the eggs; cook, without stirring, until set, 1 minute. Flip and cook 30 seconds, then transfer to a cutting board and cut into strips.

3. Heat the remaining 2 tablespoons vegetable oil in the skillet. Add the pork and stir-fry until golden but not fully cooked, about 2 minutes. Transfer to a plate. Add the scallions, ginger and garlic to the skillet and stir-fry 30 seconds. Add the broccoli slaw and bell pepper and stir-fry 4 more minutes.

4. Return the pork to the skillet and add the noodles, the reserved cooking water and the remaining soy sauce mixture. Cook, stirring, until the pork is cooked through, about 2 more minutes. Stir in the egg.

Per serving: Calories 454; Fat 20 g (Saturated 5 g); Cholesterol 153 mg; Sodium 630 mg; Carbohydrate 44 g; Fiber 7 g; Protein 28 g

Apple Pork Chops with Garlic Potatoes

Gluten-Free

SERVES 4

ACTIVE: 30 min

TOTAL: 30 min

- 1 pound small fingerling potatoes
- 2 cloves garlic
  Kosher salt
- 4 ½-inch-thick boneless pork chops (5 ounces each)
- 2 teaspoons chopped fresh sage
  Freshly ground pepper
- 1 tablespoon extra-virgin olive oil
- 1 large red onion, cut into ½-inch wedges
- 2 Granny Smith apples, cut into ½-inch pieces
- ¾ cup apple cider
- ¼ cup buttermilk

To make low-fat mashed potatoes, use a mix of buttermilk and some of the potato-cooking liquid instead of cream or milk and butter.

1. Put the potatoes and garlic in a saucepan, cover with cold water and season with salt. Cover and bring to a boil, then uncover and continue cooking until tender, about 15 minutes. Cover and set aside.

2. Meanwhile, rub the pork chops on both sides with the sage and season with salt and pepper. Heat a large cast-iron skillet over high heat, then add 1 teaspoon olive oil and sear the chops until golden on both sides, about 5 minutes total. Transfer to a plate. Wipe out the skillet and add the remaining 2 teaspoons olive oil. Add the red onion and apples and cook over medium-high heat until lightly browned, about 5 minutes. Season with salt and pepper and stir in the cider.

3. Return the chops to the skillet. Cover and cook, turning once, until just cooked through, 4 to 5 minutes. Drain the potatoes, reserving ¼ cup cooking liquid. Return the potatoes to the pan; add the buttermilk and mash, adding the reserved cooking liquid as needed. Season with salt and pepper. Serve with the pork chops, onion and apples. Drizzle with the pan juices.

Per serving: Calories 413; Fat 16 g (Saturated 5 g); Cholesterol 76 mg; Sodium 98 mg; Carbohydrate 40 g; Fiber 5 g; Protein 26 g

Pork Steaks with Zucchini Couscous

SERVES 4

ACTIVE: 35 min
TOTAL: 40 min

1 cup whole-wheat couscous

½ cup nonfat plain Greek yogurt

Hot sauce, to taste

Kosher salt

1 large pork tenderloin (about 1¼ pounds)

3 tablespoons extra-virgin olive oil

1 small clove garlic, finely grated

Freshly ground pepper

2 medium zucchini, quartered lengthwise

1 large tomato, chopped

1 tablespoon fresh lemon juice

¼ cup chopped fresh parsley

These pork "steaks" are just a butterflied pork tenderloin, cut into pieces. Butterflying a piece of meat means splitting it down the middle without cutting all the way through; the result is a thinner piece of meat that will cook more quickly.

1. Preheat a grill to medium. Cook the couscous as the label directs. Mix the yogurt, hot sauce, 1 tablespoon water, and salt to taste in a small bowl.

2. Butterfly the pork: Slice almost in half lengthwise, stopping about ½ inch from the other side, then open like a book. Cover with plastic wrap and pound with a meat mallet or heavy-bottomed skillet until the pork is a little less than ½ inch thick. Remove the plastic. Mix 1 tablespoon olive oil, the garlic, ½ teaspoon salt, and pepper to taste, then rub all over the pork.

3. Toss the zucchini with ½ tablespoon olive oil, ¼ teaspoon salt, and pepper to taste. Grill, turning once, until lightly charred, about 3 minutes per side. Transfer to a cutting board and chop.

4. Grill the pork, turning once, until just cooked through, about 3 minutes per side. Transfer to a cutting board and let rest 5 minutes.

5. Toss the couscous, zucchini, tomato, lemon juice, parsley and the remaining 1½ tablespoons olive oil in a bowl; season with salt and pepper. Cut the pork into 4 pieces and serve with the couscous and yogurt sauce.

Per serving: Calories 417; Fat 16 g (Saturated 3 g); Cholesterol 92 mg; Sodium 454 mg; Carbohydrate 31 g; Fiber 5 g; Protein 37 g

Pork and Wild Rice Salad

Gluten-Free

SERVES 4

ACTIVE: 30 min
TOTAL: 35 min

- ½ cup converted wild rice blend, flavor packet discarded
- 3 medium carrots, sliced
- ¼ teaspoon ground cinnamon
- 2 tablespoons apple cider vinegar

  Kosher salt and freshly ground pepper
- 1 large pork tenderloin (about 1¼ pounds), cut into 4 pieces
- 2 tablespoons extra-virgin olive oil
- ½ cup low-fat plain yogurt
- ¼ cup pecans, toasted and finely chopped
- 1 small clove garlic, finely grated
- 12 cups mixed baby greens (about 8 ounces)
- ⅓ cup dried cranberries or dried cherries

Converted or parboiled rice has been partially cooked, then dried and packaged, so it cooks in a fraction of the time.

1. Preheat the oven to 400°. Bring a pot of water to a boil, add the rice and cook until tender, 15 to 20 minutes. Drain; rinse under cold water.

2. Meanwhile, toss the carrots with the cinnamon, 1 tablespoon vinegar, and salt and pepper to taste in a bowl. Sprinkle the pork with ¼ teaspoon each salt and pepper. Heat the olive oil in a large ovenproof skillet over medium-high heat. Add the pork and brown on all sides, about 5 minutes. Add the carrots and cook 2 minutes. Transfer the skillet to the oven; roast until a thermometer inserted into the pork registers 150°, 8 to 10 minutes. Transfer the pork to a cutting board and let rest at least 5 minutes.

3. Whisk the yogurt, pecans, garlic, the remaining 1 tablespoon vinegar, 1 tablespoon water, ¼ teaspoon salt, and pepper to taste in a large bowl. Stir in the roasted carrots and pan drippings. Add the greens, dried cranberries and rice and toss. Season with salt and pepper and divide among plates. Slice the pork and add to the salads.

Per serving: Calories 433; Fat 16 g (Saturated 3 g); Cholesterol 76 mg; Sodium 413 mg; Carbohydrate 42 g; Fiber 8 g; Protein 32 g

Cajun Pork Chops with Kale and Beans

Gluten-Free

SERVES 4

ACTIVE: 35 min

TOTAL: 40 min

- 2 tablespoons extra-virgin olive oil
- 3 tablespoons chili powder
- 1 tablespoon jalapeño hot sauce
- 2 pounds thin-cut bone-in pork chops (about 6 chops)
- Kosher salt
- 4 stalks celery, chopped
- 1 large white onion, chopped
- 3 cloves garlic, chopped
- 2 cups low-sodium chicken broth
- 1 14.5-ounce can no-salt-added diced tomatoes
- 1 15-ounce can no-salt-added white beans, drained and rinsed
- 1 5-ounce package chopped kale (about 6 cups packed)

When shopping for pork chops, the redder the better: Pick rosy-colored pork with creamy (not yellow) fat throughout.

1. Preheat the broiler. Whisk 1 tablespoon each olive oil, chili powder and hot sauce in a bowl. Season the pork chops with ½ teaspoon salt. Pierce the chops all over with a fork and rub with the spice mixture on both sides; place on a rack set over a baking sheet. Set aside.

2. Heat the remaining 1 tablespoon olive oil in a Dutch oven or large pot over medium-high heat. Add the celery, onion, garlic and the remaining 2 tablespoons chili powder. Cook, stirring, until the vegetables are translucent, about 8 minutes.

3. Add the chicken broth and tomatoes to the pot. Cook, stirring occasionally, until reduced by about one-third, about 7 minutes. Add the beans and kale; toss to coat. Reduce the heat to medium, cover and cook until the kale is tender, about 7 minutes. (Add up to ½ cup water if the mixture looks dry.) Season with salt.

4. Meanwhile, broil the pork chops until browned, 4 to 6 minutes. Flip and broil until cooked through, 2 more minutes. Serve with the kale and beans.

Per serving: Calories 457; Fat 22 g (Saturated 6 g); Cholesterol 94 mg; Sodium 706 mg; Carbohydrate 28 g; Fiber 7 g; Protein 35 g

Spaghetti Squash and Meatballs

SERVES 4

ACTIVE: 45 min
TOTAL: 1 hr 10 min

- 1 medium spaghetti squash (about 2 pounds)
  Kosher salt
- 3 tablespoons extra-virgin olive oil, plus more for brushing
- 2 stalks celery, chopped
- 1 medium carrot, roughly chopped
- 1 medium onion, roughly chopped
- 6 cloves garlic
- 1 cup fresh parsley
- 1 pound ground beef
- 1 pound ground pork
- 2 large eggs
- 1 cup Italian-style breadcrumbs
- 1 cup plus 3 tablespoons grated parmesan cheese
- 2 28-ounce cans tomato puree
- 2 large sprigs basil
- 1 teaspoon dried oregano

This recipe makes extra sauce and meatballs. Let both cool completely, then freeze in an airtight container for up to one month.

1. Preheat the oven to 425°. Halve the squash lengthwise and scoop out the seeds. Sprinkle the cut sides with ½ teaspoon salt, then brush both sides with olive oil. Put the squash, cut-side up, in a baking dish and cover tightly with foil. Roast 20 minutes, then uncover and continue roasting until the squash is tender, about 35 more minutes.

2. Meanwhile, make the meatballs: Brush a baking sheet with olive oil. Pulse the celery, carrot, onion, garlic and parsley in a food processor to make a paste. Transfer half of the vegetable paste to a bowl; add the beef, pork, eggs, breadcrumbs, 1 cup parmesan and 1 teaspoon salt and mix with your hands until just combined. Form into about 24 two-inch meatballs; transfer to the prepared baking sheet. Bake until firm but not cooked through, about 10 minutes.

3. Make the sauce: Heat 3 tablespoons olive oil in a large pot over medium-high heat. Add the remaining vegetable paste and cook, stirring occasionally, until it looks dry, about 5 minutes. Stir in the tomato puree; rinse each can with 1 cup water and add to the pot. Stir in the basil, oregano and 1½ teaspoons salt. Bring to a simmer, then add the meatballs and simmer until the sauce thickens and the meatballs are cooked through, 15 to 20 minutes. Remove the basil.

4. Use a fork to scrape the spaghetti squash flesh into strands; transfer to a large bowl and toss with 2 tablespoons grated parmesan. Season with salt. Divide the squash among bowls and top each with 3 meatballs, some sauce and the remaining 1 tablespoon parmesan.

Per serving: Calories 654; Fat 39 g (Saturated 12 g); Cholesterol 145 mg; Sodium 2,216 mg; Carbohydrate 42 g; Fiber 5 g; Protein 38 g

SNACK TIME!

Homemade applesauce is easier than you think—and it has much less added sugar than the standard jarred version.

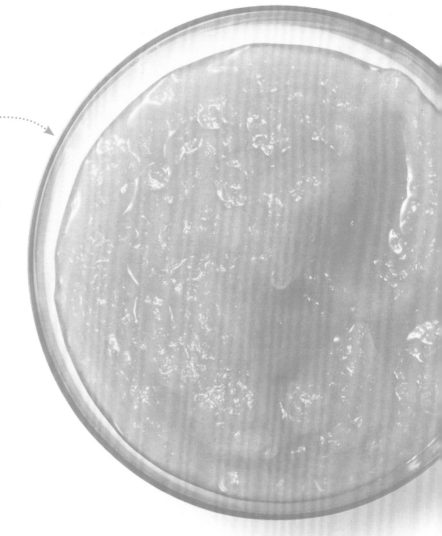

BASIC APPLESAUCE
Combine 2 pounds chopped peeled apples and ½ cup water in a saucepan; add up to 2 tablespoons sugar. Bring to a simmer, stirring occasionally; cover and cook over medium heat until the apples are very soft and most of the liquid has evaporated, 20 minutes. Add lemon juice to taste, then transfer to a blender and puree. Refrigerate until cool.

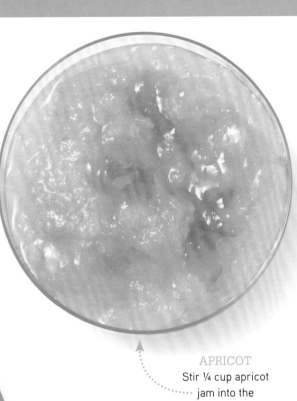

RASPBERRY
Add 1 cup raspberries
while the applesauce
is still warm; mash
slightly.

APRICOT
Stir ¼ cup apricot
jam into the
applesauce.

CRANBERRY-SPICE
Add 1 tablespoon
brown sugar,
¼ teaspoon ground
cinnamon and ½ cup
dried cranberries while
the applesauce is
still warm.

FISH
&
SEAFOOD

Tilapia Masala with Rice

Gluten-Free

SERVES 4

ACTIVE: 40 min

TOTAL: 40 min

- 1 cup basmati rice, rinsed
  Kosher salt
- ½ cup frozen peas
- ¾ cup plain yogurt
- 1 small clove garlic, chopped
- 1 1-inch piece ginger, peeled and chopped
- 1 tablespoon fresh lime juice, plus wedges for serving
- ¼ teaspoon ground cumin
- ¼ teaspoon cayenne pepper
- 4 6-ounce tilapia fillets
- 2 tablespoons unsalted butter, melted
- 1 tablespoon chopped fresh cilantro or mint

Give tilapia a try even if you're not big on fish: It's flaky and mild, and it takes on the flavor of whatever sauce you choose.

1. Bring the rice, 1⅓ cups water and ¼ teaspoon salt to a simmer in a saucepan over medium-high heat. Reduce the heat to low, cover and cook 15 minutes. Remove from the heat and add the peas; cover and set aside.

2. Combine ½ cup yogurt, the garlic, ginger, lime juice, cumin, cayenne and ¾ teaspoon salt in a food processor and process until smooth. Transfer all but 3 tablespoons of the mixture to a large bowl. Pierce the fish a few times with a fork and season with salt; add to the bowl and toss. Marinate 15 minutes.

3. Preheat the broiler. Place the fish on a broiler pan; top with the marinade and butter. Broil until opaque, 6 to 8 minutes. Mix the remaining ¼ cup yogurt, the cilantro, and salt to taste with the reserved yogurt mixture. Serve the fish and rice with the yogurt sauce and lime wedges.

Per serving: Calories 423; Fat 10 g (Saturated 5 g); Cholesterol 106 mg; Sodium 614 mg; Carbohydrate 44 g; Fiber 2 g; Protein 39 g

Niçoise Salad

Gluten-Free

SERVES 4

ACTIVE: 25 min

TOTAL: 25 min

- 1 **pound small red-skinned potatoes, quartered**
  Kosher salt
- ¾ **pound sugar snap peas, strings removed**
- 1 **cup cherry tomatoes or chopped plum tomatoes**
- 2 **tablespoons extra-virgin olive oil**
- 2 **tablespoons light mayonnaise**
- 1 **tablespoon red wine vinegar**
- 1 **head Bibb lettuce, leaves separated**
- 2 **5-ounce cans tuna packed in water, drained**
- 1 **yellow bell pepper, thinly sliced**
- 1 **tablespoon chopped pitted kalamata or niçoise olives**
- ½ **cup chopped fresh basil**
  Freshly ground pepper

When you're boiling potatoes, start them in cold salted water, then bring the water to a simmer. If you add potatoes to boiling water, the outsides will overcook before the insides are tender.

1. Put the potatoes in a medium pot and cover with water by about 2 inches. Add a pinch of salt, cover and bring to a simmer over high heat. Reduce the heat to medium high and simmer until just tender, about 5 minutes. Add the snap peas and continue simmering, covered, until the peas are crisp-tender, about 3 more minutes. Drain the potatoes and peas and rinse under cold water; transfer to a large bowl.

2. Make the dressing: Puree the tomatoes, olive oil, mayonnaise, vinegar and 1 tablespoon water in a blender.

3. Divide the lettuce among 4 bowls and drizzle with some of the dressing. Add the tuna, bell pepper, olives and basil to the potatoes and peas; add the remaining dressing and toss gently to coat. Season with salt and pepper, then pile on top of the lettuce.

Per serving: Calories 329; Fat 13 g (Saturated 2 g); Cholesterol 32 mg; Sodium 394 mg; Carbohydrate 30 g; Fiber 6 g; Protein 22 g

Soy-Glazed Salmon with Avocado Salad

SERVES 4

ACTIVE: 20 min
TOTAL: 30 min

1 tablespoon honey

2½ teaspoons low-sodium
    soy sauce

½ teaspoon cornstarch

4 6-ounce skinless center-cut
    salmon fillets (preferably wild)

1 teaspoon toasted sesame oil

    Kosher salt

2 tablespoons rice vinegar
    (not seasoned)

1 tablespoon mayonnaise

1 English cucumber, quartered
    lengthwise and sliced

3 scallions, thinly sliced

1 avocado, halved, pitted
    and chopped

    Jarred pickled ginger,
    for serving (optional)

Ask for center-cut salmon fillets at the fish counter: They're taken from the middle of the fish, which is the thickest, meatiest part.

1. Preheat the oven to 400°. Mix the honey, 2 teaspoons soy sauce and the cornstarch in a small microwave-safe bowl. Microwave until just simmering, 30 to 40 seconds.

2. Rub the fish fillets all over with ½ teaspoon sesame oil and season lightly with salt. Place the fish in a baking dish and bake 5 minutes. Remove from the oven and brush with the honey–soy sauce mixture. Return the fish to the oven and continue baking until just cooked through, 7 to 9 more minutes.

3. Meanwhile, whisk the rice vinegar, mayonnaise and the remaining ½ teaspoon each soy sauce and sesame oil in a large bowl. Add the cucumber, scallions and ¼ teaspoon salt and toss. Gently fold in the avocado. Serve the salmon with the cucumber salad and pickled ginger.

Per serving: Calories 385; Fat 18 g (Saturated 3 g); Cholesterol 98 mg; Sodium 498 mg; Carbohydrate 16 g; Fiber 5 g; Protein 39 g

Striped Bass with Artichokes and Olives

SERVES 4

ACTIVE: 20 min

TOTAL: 40 min

- 4 6-ounce skinless striped bass or other firm white fish fillets (about 1 inch thick)

  Kosher salt and freshly ground pepper

- 1 lemon
- 1 bunch parsley, leaves only (about 1 cup)
- 5 cloves garlic, smashed
- ¼ cup extra-virgin olive oil
- ½ baguette, cubed or torn
- 1 10-ounce package frozen artichoke hearts, thawed
- ½ cup pitted kalamata olives
- 3 small tomatoes, quartered

Toasted breadcrumbs taste great on fish. Make your own flavored ones by grinding leftover bread in a food processor with herbs, garlic and olive oil, then toast in the oven.

1. Position a rack in the upper third of the oven and preheat to 475°. Season the fish with salt and pepper and refrigerate until ready to use.

2. Remove the zest from the lemon using a vegetable peeler (reserve the lemon). Combine the lemon zest, parsley, garlic, 2 tablespoons olive oil and 1 teaspoon salt in a food processor. With the motor running, gradually add the bread and pulse several times to make coarse crumbs. Spread the breadcrumbs evenly in a 9-by-13-inch baking dish. Arrange the artichokes, olives and tomatoes around the edge and bake until the exposed breadcrumbs in the middle are toasted, about 15 minutes.

3. Remove the baking dish from the oven. Scoop out the toasted breadcrumbs and set aside. Add the fish to the baking dish and top with the toasted breadcrumbs. Bake until the fish is cooked through, about 15 minutes. Drizzle with the remaining 2 tablespoons olive oil. Cut the reserved lemon into wedges and squeeze on top.

Per serving: **Calories** 472; **Fat** 22 g (Saturated 3 g); **Cholesterol** 136 mg; **Sodium** 1,051 mg; **Carbohydrate** 31 g; **Fiber** 6 g; **Protein** 37 g

Salmon with Warm Tomato-Olive Salad

Gluten-Free

SERVES 4

ACTIVE: 25 min

TOTAL: 25 min

5 tablespoons extra-virgin olive oil, plus more for brushing

1 tablespoon plus 1 teaspoon red wine vinegar

1 tablespoon honey

¼ teaspoon red pepper flakes

Kosher salt

4 6-ounce salmon fillets (preferably wild), about 1¼ inches thick

1 clove garlic

½ cup coarsely chopped pitted kalamata olives

2 medium beefsteak tomatoes, cut into 1-inch chunks

1 cup sliced celery (inner stalks with leaves)

¼ cup roughly chopped fresh mint

Look for wild species of salmon at the fish counter, like sockeye, Chinook, chum, coho and pink. Much of it is from Alaska, where sustainable fishing practices are mandated in the state constitution.

1. Preheat the broiler. Line a broiler pan with foil and lightly brush with olive oil. Whisk 2 tablespoons olive oil, 1 teaspoon vinegar, the honey, red pepper flakes and 1 teaspoon salt in a small bowl. Put the salmon, skin-side down, on the prepared pan and brush the tops and sides with the honey glaze. Broil until golden brown and just cooked through, 4 to 6 minutes.

2. Meanwhile, chop the garlic; sprinkle with a generous pinch of salt, then mash into a paste with the flat side of the knife. Heat the remaining 3 tablespoons olive oil and 1 tablespoon vinegar, the olives and garlic paste in a small saucepan over medium-high heat until bubbling, about 3 minutes. Transfer the mixture to a bowl and add the tomatoes, celery and mint. Season with salt and toss to combine. Serve with the salmon.

Per serving: Calories 433; Fat 26 g (Saturated 4 g); Cholesterol 97 mg; Sodium 982 mg; Carbohydrate 10 g; Fiber 1 g; Protein 38 g

Cornmeal-Crusted Trout

Gluten-Free

SERVES 4

ACTIVE: 40 min

TOTAL: 40 min

- 1½ tablespoons unsalted butter, plus more as needed
- 1 large shallot, finely chopped
- 1 small tomato, finely chopped
- 2 tablespoons white wine vinegar
- 2 tablespoons chopped fresh tarragon

  Kosher salt and freshly ground pepper
- 8 ounces thin green beans or haricots verts
- ¾ cup cornmeal
- 8 3-ounce trout fillets, pin bones removed
- ½ cup half-and-half

To find pin bones in fish, lay a fillet over an upside-down small bowl, then run your fingers over the surface to feel for bones. Pull them out with small pliers or fish tweezers.

1. Melt ½ tablespoon butter in a skillet over medium heat. Add the shallot and cook, stirring occasionally, until just soft, about 3 minutes. Stir in the tomato, vinegar, ¼ cup water, 1 tablespoon tarragon and ¼ teaspoon each salt and pepper; bring to a simmer and cook until reduced by half, about 5 minutes. Remove from the heat.

2. Place the green beans in a large microwave-safe bowl. Drizzle with 1 tablespoon water, cover with plastic wrap and microwave until crisp-tender, about 4 minutes. Season with salt and pepper; keep warm.

3. Put the cornmeal in a shallow bowl. Dredge the fish in the cornmeal, shaking off the excess. Heat ½ tablespoon butter in a large nonstick skillet over medium-high heat. Working in batches, add the fish and cook until golden, turning once, about 5 minutes. (Add more butter between batches, if needed.) Transfer the fish to plates.

4. Return the sauce to medium heat. Add the half-and-half, bring to a simmer and cook until slightly thickened, about 3 minutes. Stir in the remaining 1 tablespoon tarragon and ½ tablespoon butter and season with salt. Serve the fish with the green beans and top with the sauce.

Per serving: Calories 380; Fat 14 g (Saturated 7 g); Cholesterol 164 mg; Sodium 238 mg; Carbohydrate 30 g; Fiber 4 g; Protein 33 g

Catfish Piccata

SERVES 4

ACTIVE: 30 min

TOTAL: 30 min

- 4 6-ounce catfish fillets
- Kosher salt and freshly ground pepper
- All-purpose flour, for dredging
- 2 tablespoons unsalted butter
- 3 tablespoons extra-virgin olive oil
- 2 cloves garlic, finely chopped
- ½ cup dry white wine
- 1 lemon (½ zested and juiced, ½ cut into wedges)
- 3 cups mixed salad greens
- 2 tablespoons capers, drained and rinsed
- ½ cup fresh parsley

Cook the catfish in a mix of butter and olive oil: You'll still get that buttery taste, but you'll keep the cholesterol in check.

1. Pat the fish dry and season with salt and pepper. Put the flour in a shallow bowl. Dredge the fish in the flour, shaking off the excess. Heat 1 tablespoon each butter and olive oil in a large nonstick skillet over medium-high heat. Add the fish and cook, turning once, until opaque, about 3 minutes per side. Transfer to a plate and cover with foil.

2. Add the garlic to the skillet and cook, stirring, until just golden, about 30 seconds. Remove from the heat and add the wine, lemon zest and lemon juice. Return to the heat and cook, stirring, until the wine is slightly reduced, about 2 minutes. Season with salt and pepper.

3. Meanwhile, toss the greens with 1 tablespoon olive oil, and salt and pepper to taste. Divide the fish among plates. Add the remaining 1 tablespoon butter to the sauce in the skillet and stir until melted. Pour the butter sauce over the fish. Wipe out the skillet.

4. Heat the remaining 1 tablespoon olive oil in the skillet over high heat. Add the capers and parsley and fry until crisp, about 1 minute; sprinkle over the fish. Serve with the salad and lemon wedges.

Per serving: Calories 402; Fat 27 g (Saturated 8 g); Cholesterol 82 mg; Sodium 464 mg; Carbohydrate 10 g; Fiber 2 g; Protein 24 g

Lemon Salmon with Lima Beans

Gluten-Free

SERVES 4

ACTIVE: 25 min

TOTAL: 40 min

- 1 lemon, halved
- ½ cup nonfat plain Greek yogurt
- ¾ teaspoon paprika
- 2 teaspoons extra-virgin olive oil
- 3 cloves garlic, thinly sliced
- ¾ teaspoon dried oregano
- Pinch of red pepper flakes
- 1 1-pound bag frozen baby lima beans
- Kosher salt and freshly ground pepper
- 2 tablespoons chopped fresh parsley
- 4 5-ounce skinless center-cut salmon fillets (preferably wild)

Lima beans are packed with fiber, iron and protein, and they're especially good when you buy them frozen. They're bright green and buttery tasting—nothing like the olive-colored, mushy canned ones you ate as a kid.

1. Slice 1 lemon half into 4 thin rounds and set aside. Grate the zest of the other lemon half and set aside; squeeze some of the juice into a bowl and mix in the yogurt and ¼ teaspoon paprika.

2. Preheat the broiler. Heat 1 teaspoon olive oil in a medium saucepan over medium heat. Add the garlic, oregano and red pepper flakes and cook until the garlic is golden, about 2 minutes. Add the lima beans, 1½ cups water and the lemon zest; partially cover the pan, bring to a simmer and cook until the beans are tender, about 20 minutes. Season with salt and pepper. Remove from the heat and stir in the parsley, 1 tablespoon of the yogurt mixture and the remaining 1 teaspoon olive oil.

3. Meanwhile, mix the remaining ½ teaspoon paprika, ½ teaspoon salt, and pepper to taste in a small bowl. Sprinkle all over the salmon; arrange on a foil-lined baking sheet and top each fillet with a lemon slice. Broil until just cooked through, 6 to 8 minutes. Serve with the lima beans and top with the yogurt mixture.

Per serving: Calories 340; Fat 8 g (Saturated 1 g); Cholesterol 81 mg; Sodium 655 mg; Carbohydrate 25 g; Fiber 7 g; Protein 40 g

Arctic Char with Mushrooms

Gluten-Free

SERVES 4

ACTIVE: 25 min

TOTAL: 25 min

- 4 6-ounce skinless arctic char fillets (about 1 inch thick)
- Kosher salt and freshly ground pepper
- ¼ cup extra-virgin olive oil, plus more for drizzling
- 8 ounces white button mushrooms, sliced
- 2 shallots, finely chopped
- 2 tablespoons red wine vinegar, plus more for drizzling
- 2 teaspoons whole-grain mustard
- 1 tablespoon chopped fresh chives
- 1 tablespoon chopped fresh parsley
- 2 bunches arugula, trimmed

Arctic char is similar to salmon, but it's a little leaner and less fishy tasting.

1. Preheat the oven to 350°. Season the fish with salt and pepper. Heat 1 tablespoon olive oil in a large nonstick skillet over medium-high heat until shimmering. Add the fish and sear until golden on the bottom and cooked halfway through, about 3 minutes. Flip onto a baking sheet, seared-side up, and bake until cooked through, 3 to 5 more minutes.

2. Meanwhile, wipe out the skillet, return to medium-high heat and add the remaining 3 tablespoons olive oil. Add the mushrooms and cook, without stirring, until browned on one side, about 1 minute. Stir and cook until browned all over, about 3 more minutes. Add the shallots and cook until soft, stirring, about 2 minutes. Whisk in 2 tablespoons vinegar and the mustard and bring to a boil. Remove from the heat and stir in the chives and parsley.

3. Drizzle the arugula with oil and vinegar in a bowl, season with salt and pepper and toss. Divide among plates and serve with the fish. Spoon the mushrooms and pan juices on top.

Per serving: Calories 376; Fat 19 g (Saturated 3 g); Cholesterol 80 mg; Sodium 399 mg; Carbohydrate 14 g; Fiber 1 g; Protein 38 g

Foil-Packet Fish with Corn Relish

Gluten-Free

SERVES 4

ACTIVE: 25 min

TOTAL: 35 min

1 teaspoon coriander seeds

1 cup fresh parsley

1 cup fresh cilantro, plus more for topping

1 1-inch piece ginger, peeled and roughly chopped

2 tablespoons vegetable oil

Kosher salt

1¾ cups corn kernels (thawed if frozen)

2 medium tomatoes, cut into chunks

4 6-ounce skinless striped bass fillets (about 1 inch thick)

2 limes, cut into wedges

This is an easy make-ahead meal: Prep the foil packets in the morning, throw them in the fridge, then put them straight on the grill later that night.

1. Preheat a grill to high. Toast the coriander seeds in a dry skillet over medium-high heat, tossing, about 3 minutes. Crush the seeds on a cutting board (the bottom of a measuring cup works well), then pulse with the parsley, cilantro, ginger, vegetable oil, ½ teaspoon salt and 1 tablespoon water in a food processor to make a coarse mixture.

2. Toss the corn and tomatoes with 2 teaspoons of the herb mixture in a bowl and season with salt.

3. Tear off 4 large sheets (about 16 inches long) of heavy-duty foil. Place a piece of fish in the center of each. (If the ends of the fillets are thin, tuck them under.) Top with a spoonful of the remaining herb mixture and surround with the corn-tomato relish. Fold up the ends of the foil and seal into packets, leaving room inside for heat circulation.

4. Grill the foil packets, covered, until the fish is just cooked through, 8 to 10 minutes. Carefully open the packets and slide the fish and vegetables onto plates. Top with more cilantro and serve with lime wedges.

Per serving: Calories 323; Fat 12 g (Saturated 2 g); Cholesterol 140 mg; Sodium 383 mg; Carbohydrate 21 g; Fiber 4 g; Protein 34 g

Steamed Fish with Ginger

SERVES 4

ACTIVE: 30 min
TOTAL: 40 min

1 1-inch piece ginger, peeled and cut into matchsticks

2 cloves garlic, thinly sliced

6 scallions, sliced

4 6-ounce skin-on striped bass or halibut fillets (or other firm white fish)

Kosher salt and freshly ground pepper

4 teaspoons toasted sesame oil

Pinch of sugar

1 to 2 tablespoons soy sauce

2 tablespoons Chinese rice wine or dry sherry

⅓ pound snow peas, trimmed

2 tablespoons peanut or vegetable oil

Steaming is an ultra-healthy way to cook fish. Put the fish on a plate that fits inside your steamer basket—the plate will catch all the flavorful juices.

1. Set a large bamboo or metal steamer basket in a skillet of simmering water over medium heat.

2. Crush the ginger slices with the flat side of a knife. Place the garlic and half each of the ginger and scallions on a plate that will fit inside the steamer. Score the fish skin a few times with a knife; season with salt and pepper. Place the fish skin-side up on the plate, drizzle with 2 teaspoons sesame oil and sprinkle with the sugar. Put the plate in the steamer. Mix the soy sauce and rice wine and pour over the fish.

3. Cover and steam the fish until just cooked through, 6 to 12 minutes, depending on the thickness. Carefully remove the hot plate. Add the snow peas to the steamer, season with salt, cover and cook until bright green, 1 to 2 minutes.

4. Transfer the fish to a platter, spoon the juices on top and sprinkle with the remaining scallions. Heat the remaining 2 teaspoons sesame oil and the peanut oil in a skillet over high heat. Add the remaining ginger and cook until it begins to brown. Pour the hot oil over the fish.

Per serving: Calories 308; Fat 15 g (Saturated 3 g); Cholesterol 74 mg; Sodium 395 mg; Carbohydrate 5 g; Fiber 1 g; Protein 35 g

Shrimp and Broccolini Stir-Fry

SERVES 4

ACTIVE: 25 min

TOTAL: 35 min

1¼ to 1½ cups grain-and-rice blend

1 tablespoon coconut oil

12 ounces large shrimp, peeled and deveined

1 red jalapeño pepper, seeded and thinly sliced

1 tablespoon grated peeled ginger

Kosher salt

2 bunches broccolini (about 1 pound), roughly chopped

3 scallions, thinly sliced

¾ cup coconut water

2 tablespoons crunchy peanut butter

2 tablespoons chopped fresh cilantro

Juice of 1 lime

Coconut water is not just for drinking! Try using it in place of regular water to cook rice or vegetables, like we did here, or to poach chicken or marinate beef. The coconut adds a subtle sweetness.

1. Cook the grain blend as the label directs; set aside.

2. Heat the coconut oil in a large nonstick skillet over medium-high heat. Add the shrimp and cook until they just turn pink, about 1 minute per side; transfer to a plate and set aside. Add the jalapeño, ginger and ½ teaspoon salt to the skillet and cook until the jalapeño softens slightly, about 1 minute. Add the broccolini and scallions and cook, stirring occasionally, until slightly softened, 2 minutes.

3. Add the coconut water to the skillet and cook, stirring, until the broccolini is just tender, about 2 minutes. Add the peanut butter and cook, stirring, until the sauce thickens slightly, about 1 minute.

4. Return the shrimp to the skillet; cook until opaque and the sauce thickens, about 2 more minutes. Stir in the cilantro and lime juice. Serve the stir-fry over the grains.

Per serving: Calories 413; Fat 13 g (Saturated 4 g); Cholesterol 129 mg; Sodium 498 mg; Carbohydrate 44 g; Fiber 14 g; Protein 31 g

Shrimp Tacos with Mango Slaw

Gluten-Free

SERVES 4
(plus extra slaw)

ACTIVE: 30 min
TOTAL: 30 min

- 3 tablespoons mayonnaise
- 1 teaspoon Sriracha or other Asian chile sauce, plus more for serving
- 2 limes (1 juiced, 1 cut into wedges)
- ½ teaspoon sugar
- ¾ cup fresh cilantro
- ¾ pound medium shrimp, peeled, deveined and halved crosswise
- 1 14-ounce package shredded coleslaw mix
- 1 mango, peeled and sliced into thin strips
- ½ small red onion, thinly sliced
  Kosher salt
- 2 teaspoons vegetable oil
- 12 hard taco shells or soft corn tortillas, warmed

To devein shrimp, make a shallow incision along the curved back with a paring knife. Slide the tip of your knife under the vein (the shrimp's digestive tract) and gently lift it out, then rinse the shrimp.

1. Make the dressing: Combine the mayonnaise, Sriracha, lime juice, sugar, ¼ cup cilantro and 1 tablespoon water in a mini food processor and pulse until smooth. (Or finely chop the cilantro and mix with the rest of the ingredients in a bowl.) Place the shrimp in a bowl and toss with 2 tablespoons of the dressing; set aside.

2. Roughly chop the remaining ½ cup cilantro. Toss with the coleslaw mix, mango, red onion and the remaining dressing. Season with salt.

3. Heat the vegetable oil in a large nonstick skillet over medium-high heat. Add the shrimp and cook, stirring occasionally, until opaque, about 3 minutes. Transfer the shrimp to a plate.

4. Fill the taco shells with the shrimp and some slaw. Serve with the lime wedges and more Sriracha. Refrigerate any extra slaw for up to 3 days.

Per serving: Calories 443; Fat 26 g (Saturated 4 g); Cholesterol 30 mg; Sodium 131 mg; Carbohydrate 50 g; Fiber 5 g; Protein 7 g

Asian Noodles with Shrimp and Edamame

SERVES 4

ACTIVE: 25 min

TOTAL: 25 min

- 10 ounces soba (buckwheat) noodles
- 1 10-ounce package frozen shelled edamame
- 1 clove garlic
- 1 1-inch piece ginger, peeled and roughly chopped
- 1½ teaspoons Sriracha (Asian chile sauce)
- 2 tablespoons vegetable oil
- Juice of 1 lime or lemon
- 2 teaspoons low-sodium soy sauce
- 1½ teaspoons toasted sesame oil, plus more for drizzling (optional)
- ½ pound medium or large shrimp, peeled and deveined, tails intact
- Kosher salt
- ¼ cup chopped fresh cilantro and/or scallions

Soba noodles are made with buckwheat, which is naturally gluten-free. If you're following a gluten-free diet, look for soba noodles that are 100% buckwheat with no added wheat flour, and use tamari instead of soy sauce—regular soy sauce contains gluten.

1. Bring a pot of water to a boil. Add the noodles and cook as the label directs, adding the edamame during the last 3 minutes of cooking. Reserve ½ cup cooking water, then drain the noodles and edamame.

2. Meanwhile, puree the garlic, ginger, Sriracha, ½ tablespoon vegetable oil and 2 tablespoons water in a blender. Mix the lime juice, soy sauce and sesame oil in a small bowl.

3. Heat the remaining 1½ tablespoons vegetable oil in a large skillet over medium-high heat. Pat the shrimp dry and season with salt; add to the pan and cook, turning, until just pink, 2 minutes. Add the Sriracha mixture and cook, stirring occasionally, until the shrimp are cooked through, about 2 more minutes.

4. Add the soy sauce mixture, noodles and edamame, herbs and the reserved cooking water to the skillet and toss. Divide among bowls and drizzle with more sesame oil.

Per serving: Calories 485; Fat 14 g (Saturated 1 g); Cholesterol 86 mg; Sodium 483 mg; Carbohydrate 64 g; Fiber 8 g; Protein 27 g

Lemon-Garlic Shrimp and Grits

Gluten-Free

SERVES 4

ACTIVE: 20 min

TOTAL: 20 min

- ¾ cup instant grits
- Kosher salt and freshly ground black pepper
- ¼ cup grated parmesan cheese
- 3 tablespoons unsalted butter
- 1¼ pounds medium shrimp, peeled and deveined, tails intact
- 2 large cloves garlic, minced
- Pinch of cayenne pepper (optional)
- Juice of ½ lemon, plus wedges for serving
- 2 tablespoons roughly chopped fresh parsley

Grits are ground dried hulled corn kernels. They typically cook for a long time, but instant grits are done in just a few minutes—perfect for weeknight meals.

1. Bring 3 cups water to a boil in a saucepan over high heat, covered. Uncover and slowly whisk in the grits, 1 teaspoon salt and ½ teaspoon pepper. Reduce the heat to medium low and cook, stirring occasionally, until thickened, about 5 minutes. Stir in the parmesan and 1 tablespoon butter. Remove from the heat and season with salt and pepper. Cover to keep warm.

2. Meanwhile, season the shrimp with salt and pepper. Melt the remaining 2 tablespoons butter in a large skillet over medium-high heat. Add the shrimp, garlic and cayenne, if using, and cook, tossing, until the shrimp are pink, 3 to 4 minutes. Remove from the heat and add 2 tablespoons water, the lemon juice and parsley; stir to coat the shrimp with the sauce and season with salt and pepper.

3. Divide the grits among shallow bowls and top with the shrimp and sauce. Serve with lemon wedges.

Per serving: Calories 367; Fat 12 g (Saturated 7 g); Cholesterol 309 mg; Sodium 904 mg; Carbohydrate 26 g; Fiber 1 g; Protein 34 g

Steamed Mussels with Fennel and Tomato

SERVES 4

ACTIVE: 20 min

TOTAL: 35 min

- ¼ cup extra-virgin olive oil
- 5 large cloves garlic, very thinly sliced
- 1 bulb fennel (with some fronds), halved and thinly sliced
- 2 carrots, very thinly sliced

  Kosher salt and freshly ground pepper
- ¼ cup dry vermouth or white wine
- 1 28-ounce can San Marzano plum tomatoes, crushed lightly by hand
- 2 teaspoons roughly chopped fresh tarragon
- 2 pounds mussels (preferably cultivated), scrubbed well and debearded

  Crusty bread, for serving

To prep mussels, rinse them under cold running water and rub the shells with a towel or bristle brush to get rid of any sand and grit. If you see any hairlike "beards," yank them toward the hinge of the shell to remove.

1. Heat the olive oil in a Dutch oven over medium heat. Add the garlic and fennel; cook until just soft and fragrant, about 4 minutes. Add the carrots and season with salt and pepper; continue cooking, stirring occasionally, until the carrots are just soft, about 4 minutes. Add the vermouth and boil to reduce slightly. Add the tomatoes and tarragon, then cover the pot and simmer until the vegetables are tender, about 15 minutes.

2. Stir in ½ cup water and the mussels. Increase the heat to high, cover and cook until the mussels open, 3 to 5 minutes. (Check halfway through and transfer any open mussels to a serving bowl.) Transfer all the mussels to a serving bowl, discarding any that do not open. Season the sauce with salt and pepper and pour over the mussels. Serve with bread.

Per serving: Calories 425; Fat 19 g; Cholesterol 65 mg; Sodium 1,220 mg; Carbohydrate 30 g; Fiber 6 g; Protein 30 g

Scallops with Brown Butter and Cabbage

Gluten-Free

SERVES 4

ACTIVE: 20 min

TOTAL: 35 min

- 1 stick unsalted butter
- 2 tablespoons packed light brown sugar
- ½ head green cabbage, sliced
- Kosher salt
- 1 cup low-sodium chicken broth
- 1¼ pounds sea scallops, "foot" muscles removed
- Freshly ground pepper
- 1 to 2 tablespoons capers, rinsed if packed in salt
- ¼ cup golden raisins
- 3 tablespoons apple cider vinegar
- ½ cup roughly chopped fresh parsley

Use a light-colored skillet to make the sauce for these scallops: Butter can go from browned to burned quickly, so you'll need to keep an eye on it!

1. Melt 2 tablespoons butter in a large skillet over medium-high heat. Sprinkle in the brown sugar and cook until it just turns golden. Add the cabbage and ½ teaspoon salt, cover and cook until wilted, about 5 minutes. Add the broth and continue cooking, covered, until crisp-tender, about 15 more minutes. Preheat the broiler.

2. Transfer the cabbage to a casserole dish. Wipe out the skillet, then add the remaining 6 tablespoons butter and melt over medium heat. Brush the scallops with some of the butter and season with salt and pepper; arrange in a single layer over the cabbage in the casserole dish and broil until firm, 5 to 7 minutes.

3. Meanwhile, continue cooking the butter over low heat, swirling the pan occasionally, until browned and fragrant, 5 minutes. Add the capers, raisins and vinegar (be careful—the butter may foam and bubble); swirl the pan until the raisins are plump. Season with salt and pepper.

4. Divide the scallops and cabbage among plates. Add the parsley to the sauce and spoon over the scallops.

Per serving: **Calories** 420; **Fat** 23 g (Saturated 14 g); **Cholesterol** 108 mg; **Sodium** 599 mg; **Carbohydrate** 25 g; **Fiber** 3 g; **Protein** 27 g

Baked Fish and Chips

SERVES 4

ACTIVE: 30 min
TOTAL: 45 min

FOR THE CHIPS

3 medium russet potatoes
(1¼ pounds)

¼ cup extra-virgin olive oil

Pinch of cayenne pepper

Kosher salt

FOR THE FISH

Olive oil cooking spray

2¾ cups crispy rice cereal

Kosher salt and freshly
ground black pepper

3 large egg whites

1½ pounds skinless, boneless
pollock fillets (or other firm
white fish), cut into
2-by-4-inch pieces

Tartar sauce and/or malt
vinegar, for serving (optional)

Try our fat-free version of tartar sauce: Mix ⅔ cup nonfat Greek yogurt and 3 tablespoons sweet pickle relish with a splash each of lemon juice and hot sauce; season with salt. Cover and chill 10 minutes.

1. Position racks in the upper and lower thirds of the oven and preheat to 450° using the convection setting, if available. Place a baking sheet on one of the racks to preheat.

2. Prepare the chips: Cut the potatoes into ¼-inch-thick sticks. Toss with the olive oil and cayenne in a bowl. Carefully remove the hot baking sheet from the oven, add the potatoes and spread in an even layer. Use a rubber spatula to scrape any oil from the bowl over the potatoes. Bake on the top oven rack, turning once, until browned and crisp, 25 to 30 minutes. Season with salt.

3. Meanwhile, make the fish: Set a wire rack on a baking sheet and coat with cooking spray. Lightly crush the cereal in a bowl with your fingers. Add 2 teaspoons salt, and black pepper to taste. In another bowl, whisk the egg whites and a pinch of salt until frothy.

4. Dip the fish in the egg whites, then roll in the cereal crumbs to coat. Place the fish pieces on the rack and mist with cooking spray.

5. Bake the fish on the bottom oven rack until crisp and just cooked through, about 12 minutes. Season with salt and black pepper. Serve the fish and chips with tartar sauce and/or malt vinegar.

Per serving: Calories 442; Fat 15 g (Saturated 2 g); Cholesterol 63 mg; Sodium 1,015 mg; Carbohydrate 37 g; Fiber 2 g; Protein 37 g

SNACK TIME!

Food is much more fun when it's on a stick! These kid-friendly combos are great for parties or after-school snacking.

HUMMUSWICHES
Sandwich toasted white bread with hummus; cut into pieces. Skewer with chopped cucumbers and cherry tomatoes.

TACO PINWHEELS
Layer sliced cheese and guacamole on sun-dried-tomato tortillas. Cut into pieces and skewer.

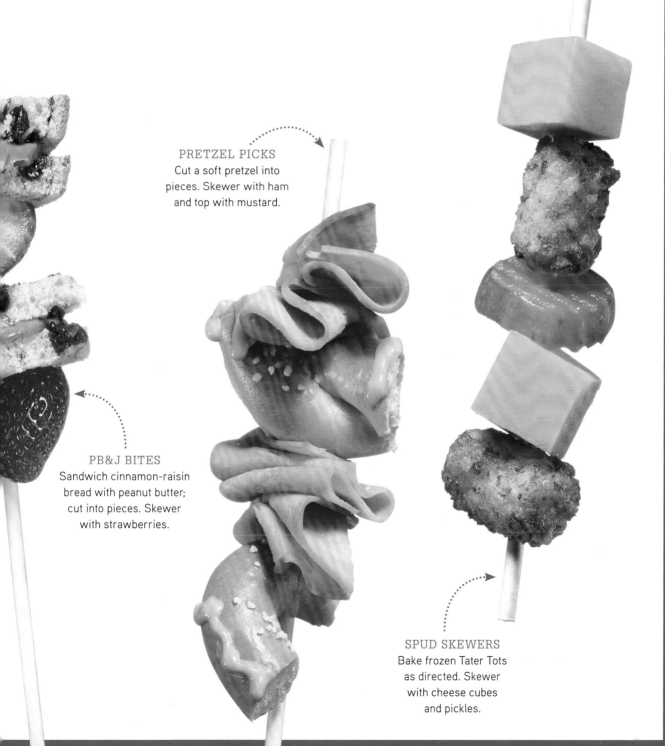

PRETZEL PICKS
Cut a soft pretzel into
pieces. Skewer with ham
and top with mustard.

PB&J BITES
Sandwich cinnamon-raisin
bread with peanut butter;
cut into pieces. Skewer
with strawberries.

SPUD SKEWERS
Bake frozen Tater Tots
as directed. Skewer
with cheese cubes
and pickles.

EGGS, TOFU
&
BEANS

Feta-and-Cauliflower Frittata

Vegetarian | Gluten-Free

SERVES 4

ACTIVE: 20 min

TOTAL: 40 min

10 large eggs

¼ cup milk

Pinch of cayenne pepper

Kosher salt and freshly ground black pepper

4 ounces feta cheese, crumbled

2 tablespoons chopped fresh dill, plus more for topping

3 tablespoons extra-virgin olive oil

½ head cauliflower, thinly sliced (about 5 cups)

6 cups mixed salad greens (about 5 ounces)

1 teaspoon white wine vinegar

You don't need to serve a frittata hot out of the oven—it's just as good at room temperature or even cold from the fridge the next day.

1. Preheat the oven to 350°. Whisk the eggs, milk and cayenne in a bowl; add 1 teaspoon salt, and black pepper to taste. Fold in the cheese and dill.

2. Heat 1 tablespoon olive oil in an ovenproof 6-to-8-inch nonstick skillet over medium-low heat, swirling to coat the pan. Add the cauliflower, ¼ teaspoon salt, and black pepper to taste; cook until the cauliflower is crisp-tender, about 5 minutes. Pour the egg mixture into the skillet and stir gently with a rubber spatula to distribute the cauliflower. Cook until the bottom is just set but not brown, about 4 minutes. Transfer the skillet to the oven and bake until the frittata is almost set on top, about 15 minutes. Remove from the oven, cover and set aside 5 minutes to finish cooking.

3. Season the greens with salt and black pepper and toss with the remaining 2 tablespoons olive oil and the vinegar. Slide the frittata onto a cutting board and slice into wedges. Sprinkle generously with dill; serve with the salad.

Per serving: **Calories** 386; **Fat** 28 g (**Saturated** 10 g); **Cholesterol** 565 mg; **Sodium** 1,129 mg; **Carbohydrate** 12 g; **Fiber** 4 g; **Protein** 22 g

Crustless Spinach Quiche

Vegetarian

SERVES 4

ACTIVE: 20 min

TOTAL: 40 min

Extra-virgin olive oil, for brushing and drizzling

4 ounces smoked gouda cheese, cut into 4 pieces

1 10-ounce package frozen spinach, thawed and squeezed dry

2 large eggs plus 2 egg whites

1 15-ounce container part-skim ricotta cheese

2 tablespoons all-purpose flour

½ teaspoon freshly grated nutmeg

6 scallions, chopped

1 tablespoon grated parmesan cheese

1 teaspoon paprika

2 heads endive, sliced lengthwise

2 tablespoons chopped walnuts

Frozen spinach can hold a lot of moisture. To keep it from watering down a dish, thaw the spinach, then wrap in a clean kitchen towel and wring dry.

1. Position a rack in the upper third of the oven, place a baking sheet on the rack and preheat to 450°. Lightly brush a 9-inch-round or 8-inch-square baking dish with olive oil.

2. Pulse the gouda in a food processor until finely chopped. Add the spinach, whole eggs and egg whites, ricotta, flour and nutmeg and process until well combined, about 30 seconds. Add the scallions and pulse to mix.

3. Pour the mixture into the prepared dish and sprinkle with the parmesan and paprika. Place the quiche on the preheated baking sheet and bake until the center is just set, 25 to 30 minutes.

4. Combine the endive and walnuts in a bowl, drizzle lightly with olive oil and toss. Serve the quiche with the endive.

Per serving: **Calories** 389; **Fat** 24 g (**Saturated** 12 g); **Cholesterol** 175 mg; **Sodium** 523 mg; **Carbohydrate** 16 g; **Fiber** 3 g; **Protein** 28 g

Egg Foo Yong

SERVES 4

ACTIVE: 35 min

TOTAL: 35 min

- 2 tablespoons vegetable oil, plus more for frying
- 6 ounces white mushrooms, trimmed and sliced
- 1½ teaspoons sugar
- 1 cup low-sodium chicken broth
- 3½ teaspoons soy sauce
- 1 tablespoon cornstarch
- ½ medium onion, thinly sliced
- 6 ounces Canadian bacon, diced
- ½ cup frozen peas, thawed
- 1 bunch scallions, thinly sliced
- 6 large eggs, beaten
- 1 teaspoon toasted sesame oil

Canadian bacon adds smoky flavor to this dish—but not a lot of fat. It's made from lean pork loin; standard bacon comes from the fattier pork belly.

1. Heat 1 tablespoon vegetable oil in a skillet over high heat. Add the mushrooms and ½ teaspoon sugar and sauté until golden, 3 minutes. Add the chicken broth and 2 teaspoons soy sauce. Mix the cornstarch with ¼ cup water in a small bowl; stir into the skillet and boil until thickened, 2 minutes. Set the gravy aside.

2. Heat 1 tablespoon vegetable oil in another skillet over high heat. Add the onion and the remaining 1 teaspoon sugar and cook until tender, 4 minutes. Add the bacon and cook 2 minutes. Add the peas, half of the scallions and the remaining 1½ teaspoons soy sauce; cook 1 more minute. Transfer to a bowl and combine with the beaten eggs.

3. Wipe out the skillet. Return to high heat and add ¼ inch of vegetable oil. Add one-quarter of the egg mixture; spoon some of the hot oil on top and cook until puffy, 1 to 2 minutes. Flip and cook 1 minute, then drain on paper towels. Repeat to make 3 more omelets. Add the sesame oil to the mushroom gravy and pour over the omelets. Top with the remaining scallions.

Per serving: **Calories** 351; **Fat** 25 g (**Saturated** 5 g); **Cholesterol** 338 mg; **Sodium** 725 mg; **Carbohydrate** 15 g; **Fiber** 2 g; **Protein** 19 g

Scrambled Eggs with Broccolini

Vegetarian

SERVES 4

ACTIVE: 20 min

TOTAL: 20 min

3 tablespoons extra-virgin olive oil

1 large bunch broccolini, roughly chopped

Kosher salt and freshly ground pepper

8 large eggs, beaten

⅓ cup ricotta cheese

¼ cup grated parmesan cheese

Crusty bread, for serving (optional)

For perfect scrambled eggs, pull the skillet from the heat when the eggs are still a little loose—they'll continue cooking even after you remove them from the pan.

1. Heat 2 tablespoons olive oil in a large nonstick skillet over medium heat. Add the broccolini, 2 tablespoons water, ¼ teaspoon salt, and pepper to taste. Cover and cook, stirring occasionally, until crisp-tender, about 6 minutes. Transfer to a bowl.

2. Add the remaining 1 tablespoon olive oil to the skillet. Add the eggs, ½ teaspoon salt, and pepper to taste and cook, stirring with a rubber spatula, until the eggs are just barely set, about 3 minutes. Remove from the heat and stir in the broccolini and ricotta. Sprinkle with the parmesan. Serve with bread.

Per serving: **Calories** 335; **Fat** 25 g (Saturated 8 g); **Cholesterol** 451 mg; **Sodium** 633 mg; **Carbohydrate** 8 g; **Fiber** 1 g; **Protein** 19 g

Polenta with Fontina and Eggs

Vegetarian | Gluten-Free

SERVES 4

ACTIVE: 25 min

TOTAL: 40 min

- 2 tablespoons plus 1 teaspoon extra-virgin olive oil
- 1 18-ounce tube prepared polenta, cut into 12 rounds
- 3 cloves garlic, finely chopped

  Pinch of red pepper flakes
- 1 15-ounce can crushed tomatoes

  Kosher salt and freshly ground pepper
- 8 large eggs
- 1 cup grated fontina cheese (about 4 ounces)
- 1 tablespoon chopped fresh parsley

Keep a tube of pre-made polenta in your pantry as an alternative to rice or pasta. Slice and brown it in a skillet for a few minutes per side, then serve with something saucy.

1. Preheat the oven to 400°. Heat 2 tablespoons olive oil in a large nonstick ovenproof skillet over medium-high heat. Pat the polenta slices dry with paper towels, add to the skillet and cook until golden, about 3 minutes per side. Transfer to a plate.

2. Reduce the heat under the skillet to low. Add the remaining 1 teaspoon olive oil, the garlic and red pepper flakes and cook until the garlic is golden, about 1 minute. Add the tomatoes and ½ cup water, bring to a simmer and cook 5 minutes; season with salt and pepper. Remove ¼ cup of the sauce and set aside.

3. Arrange the polenta rounds in the skillet with the sauce, then carefully crack the eggs on top. Season with salt and pepper and top with the reserved sauce and the cheese. Transfer to the oven and bake until the egg whites are set, 13 to 15 minutes. Top with the parsley.

Per serving: **Calories** 471; **Fat** 25 g (**Saturated** 9 g); **Cholesterol** 393 mg; **Sodium** 962 mg; **Carbohydrate** 33 g; **Fiber** 3 g; **Protein** 24 g

Spaghetti Squash Tostadas

Vegetarian | Gluten-Free

SERVES 4

ACTIVE: 25 min

TOTAL: 40 min

> 3 tablespoons vegetable oil, plus more for frying
>
> 2½ teaspoons chili powder
>
> 1 teaspoon chipotle chile powder
>
> Kosher salt and freshly ground pepper
>
> 1 pint cherry tomatoes, halved
>
> 1 large red onion, cut into ½-inch wedges
>
> ½ spaghetti squash, halved and seeded
>
> 1 15-ounce can black beans (do not drain)
>
> 8 corn tortillas
>
> ½ cup sour cream
>
> Fresh cilantro, for topping
>
> Lime wedges, for serving

No need to drain the beans for this recipe: The starchy liquid makes the tostada filling thick, creamy and super flavorful.

1. Preheat the oven to 425°. Whisk 2 tablespoons vegetable oil, 2 teaspoons chili powder, the chipotle powder, 1 teaspoon salt and a few grinds of pepper in a bowl. Add the tomatoes and red onion; toss. Roast on a baking sheet, stirring once, until tender, 25 minutes.

2. Meanwhile, put the squash cut-side up in a microwave-safe dish; add ½ cup water, cover with plastic wrap and microwave until tender, 10 to 15 minutes. Let cool; scrape the flesh into a bowl using a fork. Add the roasted vegetables and toss.

3. Heat the remaining 1 tablespoon vegetable oil and ½ teaspoon chili powder in a medium skillet over medium heat. Add the beans and mash with a fork. Bring to a simmer; cook, stirring, until thickened, about 5 minutes. Add a splash of water if the beans get too thick.

4. Heat ½ inch vegetable oil in a separate skillet over medium-high heat. Fry each tortilla until crisp, 2 minutes. Spread the beans on the tortillas; top with the vegetables, sour cream and cilantro. Serve with lime wedges.

Per serving: **Calories** 440; **Fat** 18 g (**Saturated** 5 g); **Cholesterol** 20 mg; **Sodium** 599 mg; **Carbohydrate** 59 g; **Fiber** 8 g; **Protein** 11 g

Middle Eastern Rice and Lentils

Vegetarian | Gluten-Free

SERVES 4

ACTIVE: 20 min

TOTAL: 40 min

- 2 cups shredded carrots (about 4)
- 2 tablespoons fresh lemon juice
- 2 teaspoons ground cumin
- Kosher salt and freshly ground black pepper
- ¼ cup extra-virgin olive oil
- 1 onion, halved and thinly sliced
- 2 cloves garlic, finely chopped
- ¼ teaspoon ground cinnamon
- ¼ teaspoon cayenne pepper
- 1¼ cups basmati rice
- 1 15-ounce can lentils, drained and rinsed
- ¾ cup low-fat plain Greek yogurt
- Chopped fresh cilantro, for topping

Don't skip the cinnamon in this recipe! Baking spices like cinnamon, allspice and nutmeg have been used for centuries in Middle Eastern cooking to bring out rich flavors in savory dishes.

1. Toss the carrots with the lemon juice, ¼ teaspoon each cumin and salt, and a few grinds of black pepper in a bowl; set aside.

2. Heat the olive oil in a medium saucepan over medium-high heat. Add the onion and cook, stirring often, until deep golden brown, about 12 minutes. Using a slotted spoon, remove about half of the onion to a paper towel–lined plate; set aside.

3. Add the garlic, cinnamon, cayenne and the remaining 1¾ teaspoons cumin to the pan with the remaining onion. Cook, stirring, 1 minute. Stir in the rice and ¾ teaspoon salt. Add 2½ cups water and bring to a boil. Reduce the heat to low, cover and cook until the rice is tender and the water is absorbed, about 18 minutes.

4. Stir the lentils into the rice. Serve topped with the reserved carrot mixture and onion, the yogurt and cilantro.

Per serving: **Calories** 454; **Fat** 15 g (Saturated 2 g); **Cholesterol** 0 mg; **Sodium** 654 mg; **Carbohydrate** 66 g; **Fiber** 11 g; **Protein** 14 g

Eggplant and Tofu Curry

Vegetarian | Vegan | Gluten-Free

SERVES 4

ACTIVE: 30 min

TOTAL: 30 min

- 3 tablespoons vegetable oil
- 1 medium onion, sliced
- 5 cloves garlic
- 1 3-inch piece ginger, peeled
- 1 jalapeño pepper (remove seeds for less heat)
- 1 14-ounce can whole plum tomatoes
- 2 Japanese eggplants, cut into ¾-inch pieces
- 1 teaspoon curry powder
- 1 14-ounce can unsweetened coconut milk
- 1 12-to-14-ounce package firm tofu, cut into ½-inch cubes and patted dry
- 3 cups spinach

  Kosher salt and freshly ground pepper

  Rice, for serving (optional)

If eggplant is normally too bitter for your taste, give the Japanese variety a try. Japanese eggplants have a thin skin and slightly sweet, nearly seedless flesh.

1. Heat 1 tablespoon vegetable oil in a pot over medium-high heat. Add the onion and cook until softened, about 5 minutes. Meanwhile, puree the garlic, ginger, jalapeño and 1 to 2 tablespoons water in a mini food processor until a paste forms. Drain the tomatoes, reserving the juice; coarsely crush the tomatoes in a separate bowl.

2. Add the remaining 2 tablespoons vegetable oil and the eggplant to the pot; cook 2 minutes. Add the garlic-ginger paste and cook, stirring, 2 more minutes. Add the curry powder and tomatoes (but not the juice) and cook, stirring, 1 minute. Add the tomato juice and 1 cup water and cook until slightly reduced, about 3 minutes. Add the coconut milk and tofu; simmer until the eggplant is very tender, about 5 minutes. Add the spinach and cook until wilted, about 1 minute. Season with salt and pepper. Serve with rice.

Per serving (without rice): **Calories** 435; **Fat** 38 g (**Saturated** 21 g); **Cholesterol** 0 mg; **Sodium** 91 mg; **Carbohydrate** 17 g; **Fiber** 7 g; **Protein** 14 g

Barbecue Tofu with Cajun Rice

Vegetarian | Vegan

SERVES 4

ACTIVE: 35 min
TOTAL: 40 min

- 3 tablespoons extra-virgin olive oil
- ½ onion, chopped
- 2 stalks celery, chopped
- 2 cloves garlic, minced
- 1¼ cups converted white rice
- 1 teaspoon Cajun seasoning
- Kosher salt
- 1 14-ounce package extra-firm tofu
- 2 bell peppers (1 red, 1 green), thinly sliced
- Freshly ground pepper
- ¼ cup barbecue sauce
- 2 scallions, chopped
- 3 tablespoons chopped fresh parsley

Tofu is a blank canvas—you can make it taste like whatever you want! Try your favorite barbecue sauce here; the tofu soaks up all the flavor.

1. Heat 1 tablespoon olive oil in a saucepan over medium heat. Add the onion and celery; cook, stirring, until softened, 4 minutes. Add the garlic and cook 1 minute. Add the rice and Cajun seasoning and cook, stirring, until lightly toasted, about 1 minute. Increase the heat to medium high; stir in 2 cups water and ¾ teaspoon salt. Bring to a simmer, then reduce the heat to low; cover and cook until tender, about 15 minutes. Uncover and set aside.

2. Wrap the tofu in paper towels and set on a plate. Weigh down with a bowl; let drain 10 minutes. Cut in half lengthwise, then slice ½ inch thick.

3. Heat a large nonstick skillet over medium-high heat. Add 1 tablespoon olive oil, the bell peppers, and salt and pepper to taste. Cook, stirring, until the peppers start browning, 4 minutes; transfer to a plate.

4. Add the remaining 1 tablespoon olive oil and the tofu to the skillet in a single layer. Cook until browned, about 4 minutes per side. Stir in the bell peppers, barbecue sauce and scallions. Stir the parsley into the rice; top with the tofu.

Per serving: **Calories** 450; **Fat** 16 g (**Saturated** 2 g); **Cholesterol** 0 mg; **Sodium** 650 mg; **Carbohydrate** 60 g; **Fiber** 3 g; **Protein** 15 g

Tofu-Potato Scramble

Vegetarian

SERVES 4

ACTIVE: 25 min

TOTAL: 30 min

1 large Yukon gold potato, peeled and cut into ½-inch pieces

1 tablespoon extra-virgin olive oil

1 bunch scallions, thinly sliced

2 cloves garlic, chopped

2 teaspoons chili powder

2 bell peppers (1 red, 1 green), chopped

Kosher salt

1 12-to-14-ounce package firm tofu, drained and crumbled

4 8-inch whole-wheat tortillas

¼ cup shredded part-skim mozzarella cheese

1 cup cherry tomatoes, halved

1 cup shredded lettuce

Crumbled tofu tastes like scrambled eggs in this dish. It's a great easy dinner for vegans—just skip the cheese on top.

1. Put the potato pieces in a large skillet and cover with water. Bring to a boil, then reduce the heat to medium and simmer 3 minutes. Pour out all but about 1 tablespoon of the water.

2. Add the olive oil, scallions, garlic and chili powder to the skillet with the potatoes and cook, stirring, 2 minutes. Add the bell peppers and ½ teaspoon salt and cook, stirring occasionally, until the potatoes and peppers are tender, 5 to 7 more minutes. Add the tofu and 2 tablespoons water and cook until the tofu is heated through, about 3 more minutes. Season with salt.

3. Toast the tortillas in a dry skillet, 1 minute per side, or wrap in a damp paper towel and microwave 1 minute. Divide among plates and top with the tofu scramble. Pile the cheese, cherry tomatoes and lettuce on top.

Per serving: **Calories** 374; **Fat** 16 g (**Saturated** 3 g); **Cholesterol** 4 mg; **Sodium** 626 mg; **Carbohydrate** 42 g; **Fiber** 6 g; **Protein** 19 g

Tofu Tacos
Vegetarian

SERVES 4

ACTIVE: 30 min
TOTAL: 30 min

- 1 12-to-14-ounce package firm tofu, drained and cut into 8 slices
- 4 cups shredded coleslaw mix
- 1 small bunch radishes, thinly sliced
- ½ cup chopped fresh cilantro
- 1 bunch scallions, sliced
- 1½ tablespoons extra-virgin olive oil
- 2 limes (1 zested and juiced, 1 cut into wedges)
- ¼ cup nonfat plain Greek yogurt
  Kosher salt and freshly ground pepper
- 1 tablespoon taco seasoning
- 8 8-inch whole-wheat tortillas
- ¼ cup shredded part-skim mozzarella or pepper jack cheese
- ¼ cup jarred salsa verde

For crisp, golden tofu, be sure to press out the excess water before frying. Any moisture will cause the tofu to steam instead of fry.

1. Lay the tofu slices on a stack of paper towels; top with more paper towels, then put a heavy skillet on top and let drain 10 minutes. Meanwhile, toss the coleslaw, radishes, cilantro, scallions, 1 tablespoon olive oil, the lime zest and half of the lime juice in a large bowl. Mix the yogurt with the remaining lime juice in a small bowl and season with salt and pepper.

2. Brush the tofu on all sides with the remaining ½ tablespoon olive oil and sprinkle with the taco seasoning. Heat a nonstick skillet over medium-high heat, then add the tofu and cook until it begins to crisp, about 5 minutes; flip and cook 2 more minutes. Cut into strips.

3. Toast the tortillas in a dry skillet, 1 minute per side, or wrap in a damp paper towel and microwave 1 minute. Fill with the tofu, cheese and slaw, then drizzle with the yogurt sauce and salsa. Serve with the lime wedges.

Per serving: **Calories** 481; **Fat** 19 g (Saturated 3 g); **Cholesterol** 4 mg; **Sodium** 537 mg; **Carbohydrate** 56 g; **Fiber** 8 g; **Protein** 22 g

Tofu-Vegetable Stir-Fry

Vegetarian | Vegan

SERVES 4

ACTIVE: 25 min

TOTAL: 25 min

- 1 cup white rice
- 3 tablespoons low-sodium soy sauce
- 3 tablespoons hoisin sauce
- 2 tablespoons balsamic vinegar
- 1 tablespoon Sriracha (Asian chile sauce)
- 2 teaspoons cornstarch
- 2 tablespoons toasted sesame oil
- 4 scallions, sliced (white and green parts separated)
- 2 cloves garlic, minced
- 1 1-inch piece ginger, peeled and finely chopped
- 4 ounces shiitake mushrooms, stemmed and chopped
- 4 ounces snow peas, strings removed
- 1 12-to-14-ounce package soft tofu, drained and cut into 1-inch cubes

Prep all your ingredients before you start cooking and set them by the stove: This stir-fry comes together quickly.

1. Cook the rice as the label directs. Meanwhile, whisk the soy sauce, hoisin sauce, vinegar, chile sauce, cornstarch and 1 cup water in a small bowl until smooth; set aside.

2. Heat the sesame oil in a large skillet over medium-high heat. Add the scallion whites, garlic and ginger and stir-fry 30 seconds. Add the mushrooms and stir-fry until golden brown and tender, about 3 minutes. Add the snow peas and stir-fry 30 more seconds.

3. Whisk the reserved soy sauce mixture and add it to the skillet. Bring to a simmer, then add the tofu. Cook, stirring occasionally, until the sauce is thick, about 2 minutes. Sprinkle with the scallion greens.

4. Fluff the rice with a fork and divide among bowls. Top with the stir-fry.

Per serving: **Calories** 377; **Fat** 11 g (Saturated 2 g); **Cholesterol** 0 mg; **Sodium** 992 mg; **Carbohydrate** 58 g; **Fiber** 2 g; **Protein** 13 g

SNACK TIME!

Try a new version of ants on a log!

ANTS
ON A RANCH
Mix cream cheese with ranch dressing; spread on celery and top with thawed frozen peas.

BERRIES
ON A BRANCH
Spread cookie butter on celery; top with blueberries.

LADYBUGS
ON A LOG
Spread strawberry cream cheese on celery; top with dried cranberries.

BEANS
ON A STALK
Spread guacamole
on celery; top with
black beans
(drained and
rinsed).

FISH
IN A STREAM
Spread hummus
on celery; top with
Goldfish pretzels.

PIGS IN A PEN
Spread pimiento
cheese on celery;
top with crumbled
cooked bacon.

PASTA
&
GRAINS

Spaghetti with Tuna Marinara Sauce

SERVES 4

ACTIVE: 25 min
TOTAL: 30 min

Kosher salt

1½ pounds plum tomatoes
(6 to 8 tomatoes)

2½ tablespoons extra-virgin
olive oil

3 cloves garlic, thinly sliced

¼ teaspoon red pepper flakes,
plus more to taste

½ cup dry white wine

12 ounces spaghetti

1 5-ounce can light tuna
packed in water, drained

Freshly ground pepper

½ cup roughly chopped fresh
basil

When you're using fresh basil in a sauce, add it at the very end—the leaves can turn black and lose flavor if they cook for too long.

1. Bring a large pot of salted water to a boil. Meanwhile, puree the tomatoes in a blender or food processor; set aside. Heat the olive oil in a large skillet over medium heat. Add the garlic and red pepper flakes and cook, stirring, until the garlic is just golden, about 2 minutes. Increase the heat to medium high, add the wine and cook until reduced by half, about 1 minute. Add the pureed tomatoes and ¾ teaspoon salt and simmer, stirring, until the sauce thickens slightly, about 6 more minutes. Remove from the heat and keep warm.

2. Add the pasta to the boiling water and cook as the label directs, then drain. Return the skillet with the sauce to medium heat, add the pasta and tuna and cook, tossing, 1 minute. Season with salt and pepper. Remove from the heat and stir in the basil.

Per serving: Calories 487; Fat 11 g (Saturated 2 g); Cholesterol 22 mg; Sodium 519 mg; Carbohydrate 71 g; Fiber 5 g; Protein 22 g

Rigatoni with Spicy Shrimp

SERVES 4

ACTIVE: 25 min
TOTAL: 30 min

Kosher salt

12 ounces mezzi rigatoni (or other short pasta)

1 tablespoon extra-virgin olive oil

1 pound large shrimp, peeled and deveined

½ teaspoon red pepper flakes

1 medium shallot, minced

¼ cup white wine or low-sodium chicken broth

1 15-ounce can no-salt-added diced tomatoes

½ cup chopped fresh basil

2 tablespoons heavy cream

We like the mild flavor and delicate texture of shallots, but if you don't have any on hand, you can substitute ½ red onion for every medium shallot.

1. Bring a large pot of salted water to a boil. Add the pasta and cook as the label directs. Reserve 1 cup cooking water, then drain.

2. Meanwhile, heat the olive oil in a large nonstick skillet over medium-high heat. Add the shrimp in a single layer and season with ¼ teaspoon red pepper flakes and a pinch of salt. Cook until just pink, about 2 minutes, then flip and cook until no longer translucent, 1 to 2 more minutes. Transfer to a plate.

3. Add the shallot to the skillet and cook, stirring with a wooden spoon, until translucent, about 2 minutes. Add the wine and cook, scraping up any browned bits, until slightly reduced, about 1 minute. Add the tomatoes, half of the basil, the remaining ¼ teaspoon red pepper flakes and ¼ teaspoon salt; cook until slightly thickened, about 5 minutes. Stir in the heavy cream and cook 1 more minute.

4. Return the shrimp and any collected juices to the skillet. Stir in the pasta; add enough of the reserved cooking water to loosen the sauce. Season with salt. Top with the remaining basil.

Per serving: Calories 490; Fat 9 g (Saturated 3 g); Cholesterol 178 mg; Sodium 481 mg; Carbohydrate 68 g; Fiber 4 g; Protein 31 g

Broken Lasagna with Zucchini and Tomatoes

Vegetarian

SERVES 4

ACTIVE: 20 min

TOTAL: 30 min

Kosher salt

2 large zucchini, coarsely grated

12 ounces lasagna noodles, broken into bite-size pieces

3 tablespoons unsalted butter

2 cups cherry tomatoes (1 cup whole, 1 cup halved)

½ teaspoon finely grated lemon zest

Freshly ground pepper

½ cup grated parmesan cheese (about 1 ounce), plus more for topping

1 small bunch chives, cut into 1-inch pieces

Try a new pasta shape—broken lasagna noodles—and use up the pieces left at the bottom of the box. Just make sure you don't use no-boil noodles.

1. Bring a large pot of salted water to a boil. Meanwhile, toss the zucchini with ½ teaspoon salt in a colander set over a large bowl. Let stand 10 minutes, then gently squeeze out the excess moisture.

2. Add the pasta to the boiling water and stir vigorously to prevent it from sticking. Cook until al dente, about 12 minutes. Reserve ½ cup of the cooking water, then drain the pasta.

3. Meanwhile, melt the butter in a large skillet over medium-high heat. Add the cherry tomatoes and cook until blistered and slightly softened, about 4 minutes. Stir in the zucchini and lemon zest and cook, lightly crushing the tomatoes with a wooden spoon, until the zucchini is tender, about 4 minutes. Season with salt and pepper.

4. Transfer the zucchini-tomato mixture to a large bowl. Add the pasta and cheese and toss. Stir in half of the chives and about ¼ cup of the reserved cooking water, adding more to loosen, if needed. Season with salt and pepper. Divide among bowls and top with more cheese and the remaining chives.

Per serving: Calories 478; Fat 13 g (Saturated 8 g); Cholesterol 36 mg; Sodium 407 mg; Carbohydrate 73 g; Fiber 6 g; Protein 17 g

Low-Cal Fettuccine Alfredo

Vegetarian

SERVES 4

ACTIVE: 25 min

TOTAL: 25 min

- 1 tablespoon unsalted butter
- 1 clove garlic, minced
- 1 teaspoon grated lemon zest
- 2 teaspoons all-purpose flour
- 1 cup low-fat (2%) milk
  Kosher salt
- 2 tablespoons Neufchâtel or low-fat cream cheese
- ¾ cup grated parmesan cheese (about 1½ ounces), plus more for topping
- 3 tablespoons chopped fresh parsley
- 12 ounces fresh fettuccine
  Freshly ground pepper

Traditional Alfredo sauce calls for heavy cream; to keep this recipe light, we thickened low-fat milk with flour instead, then added a little cream cheese and parmesan for richness.

1. Make the sauce: Melt the butter in a skillet over medium heat. Add the garlic and lemon zest and cook until the garlic is slightly soft, about 1 minute. Add the flour and cook, stirring with a wooden spoon, 1 minute. Whisk in the milk and ¾ teaspoon salt and cook, whisking constantly, until just thickened, about 3 minutes. Add the Neufchâtel and parmesan cheese; whisk until melted, about 1 minute. Stir in the parsley.

2. Meanwhile, bring a large pot of salted water to a boil. Add the fettuccine and cook until al dente, 2 to 3 minutes. Reserve 1 cup cooking water, then drain the pasta and return to the pot.

3. Add the sauce and ½ cup of the reserved cooking water to the pasta and gently toss, adding more cooking water as needed to loosen. Season with salt. Divide among bowls and top with more parmesan and pepper.

Per serving: Calories 490; Fat 15 g (Saturated 8 g); Cholesterol 48 mg; Sodium 734 mg; Carbohydrate 66 g; Fiber 3 g; Protein 20 g

Sicilian Cauliflower Pasta

Vegetarian

SERVES 4

ACTIVE: 20 min
TOTAL: 30 min

Kosher salt

12 ounces whole-wheat penne

½ head cauliflower

2 tablespoons extra-virgin olive oil

3 tablespoons golden raisins

1 clove garlic, finely chopped

Pinch of red pepper flakes

1 cup fresh parsley, chopped

¼ cup fresh dill, chopped

1 tablespoon fresh lemon juice

2 tablespoons grated pecorino romano or parmesan cheese, plus more for topping (optional)

Whole-wheat pasta can have a strong nutty flavor, so try to pair it with other bold ingredients. Here we used raisins, cauliflower and loads of fresh herbs.

1. Bring a large pot of salted water to a boil. Add the pasta and cook as the label directs. Reserve ¾ cup cooking water, then drain the pasta.

2. Meanwhile, trim the thick stems off the cauliflower and coarsely grate the florets on the large holes of a box grater (it's fine if some small florets remain whole). Heat the olive oil in a large skillet over medium-high heat. Add the cauliflower, raisins, garlic, red pepper flakes and ¼ teaspoon salt and cook, stirring occasionally, until the cauliflower is crisp-tender and slightly browned, about 4 minutes.

3. Remove the skillet from the heat and stir in the pasta, parsley, dill, lemon juice, cheese and ½ cup of the reserved cooking water. Add more cooking water to loosen, if needed. Season with salt. Serve with more grated cheese.

Per serving: Calories 414; Fat 10 g (Saturated 2 g); Cholesterol 4 mg; Sodium 213 mg; Carbohydrate 73 g; Fiber 13 g; Protein 16 g

Gnocchi with Squash and Kale

Vegetarian

SERVES 4

ACTIVE: 30 min
TOTAL: 35 min

- 2 tablespoons unsalted butter
- ½ medium butternut squash, peeled, seeded and cut into ½-inch pieces
- 3 cloves garlic, thinly sliced
- 1 tablespoon roughly chopped fresh sage
- ¼ teaspoon red pepper flakes
  Kosher salt
- 1¼ cups low-sodium vegetable or chicken broth
- 1 bunch kale, stemmed and roughly chopped (about 8 cups)
- 1 17.5-ounce package potato gnocchi
- ¾ cup grated parmesan or pecorino romano cheese (about 1½ ounces)

Fake a baked pasta: Toss cooked gnocchi, ravioli or other pasta with sauce in an ovenproof skillet; top with parmesan and broil until bubbly.

1. Melt 1 tablespoon butter in a large ovenproof skillet over medium heat. Add the squash and cook, stirring, until slightly soft and golden, about 8 minutes. Add the garlic, sage, red pepper flakes and 1 teaspoon salt; cook until the garlic is soft, about 2 more minutes.

2. Preheat the broiler. Add the chicken broth to the skillet. When it starts to simmer, stir in the kale and cook until it wilts slightly, about 2 minutes. Add the gnocchi, stirring to coat. Cover and cook until the gnocchi are just tender, about 5 minutes. Uncover and stir in ¼ cup parmesan and the remaining 1 tablespoon butter. Sprinkle with the remaining ½ cup parmesan; transfer to the broiler and cook until golden and bubbly, about 3 minutes.

Per serving: Calories 438; Fat 23 g (Saturated 14 g); Cholesterol 76 mg; Sodium 989 mg; Carbohydrate 42 g; Fiber 6 g; Protein 16 g

Penne with Butternut Squash
Vegetarian

SERVES 4

ACTIVE: 30 min

TOTAL: 30 min

Kosher salt

12 ounces whole-wheat or multigrain penne

2 tablespoons extra-virgin olive oil

2 cups diced peeled butternut squash (about 8 ounces)

Freshly ground pepper

12 ounces cremini mushrooms, trimmed and sliced

4 cloves garlic, minced

1 medium shallot or ½ small red onion, minced

¼ teaspoon red pepper flakes, plus more to taste

1 cup grated parmesan cheese (about 2 ounces)

3 tablespoons fresh oregano

Butternut squash is a great source of fiber and beta-carotene. Browning it, as we do here, brings out its sweetness.

1. Bring a large pot of salted water to a boil. Add the pasta and cook as the label directs; reserve 1 cup cooking water, then drain the pasta.

2. Meanwhile, heat 1 tablespoon olive oil in a large nonstick skillet over medium-high heat. Add the squash, ¼ teaspoon salt and a few grinds of pepper. Cook, stirring occasionally, until golden and tender, about 5 minutes. Transfer to a plate and set aside.

3. Add the remaining 1 tablespoon olive oil, the mushrooms, ¼ teaspoon salt and a few grinds of pepper to the skillet. Cook, stirring occasionally, until lightly browned, about 5 minutes. Add the garlic, shallot and red pepper flakes. Cook, stirring, until the shallot softens, about 2 minutes.

4. Add the pasta, squash and ½ cup of the reserved cooking water to the skillet. Cook, stirring, until heated through, 1 to 2 minutes. Stir in ½ cup parmesan, then stir in enough of the remaining cooking water to loosen. Stir in the oregano and season with salt and pepper. Top with the remaining ½ cup parmesan.

Per serving: Calories 499; Fat 14 g (Saturated 4 g); Cholesterol 18 mg; Sodium 330 mg; Carbohydrate 77 g; Fiber 9 g; Protein 17 g

Three-Cheese Macaroni

Vegetarian

SERVES 6

ACTIVE: 30 min

TOTAL: 50 min

1 large egg

1 12-ounce can evaporated whole milk

Pinch of cayenne pepper

Pinch of freshly grated nutmeg

Kosher salt and freshly ground black pepper

1⅓ cups grated muenster cheese (about 4 ounces), plus 4 deli-thin slices (about 1 ounce)

½ cup grated sharp cheddar cheese (about 2 ounces)

¼ cup grated parmesan cheese (about ½ ounce)

½ head cauliflower, cut into small florets (about 4 cups)

4 cups medium pasta shells (about 9 ounces)

You'd never know it, but this low-fat mac and cheese gets its creamy texture from pureed cauliflower!

1. Whisk the egg, evaporated milk, cayenne, nutmeg, and salt and black pepper to taste in a bowl. Toss the grated cheeses in a separate bowl.

2. Bring a large pot of salted water to a boil. Add the cauliflower and cook until almost falling apart, about 7 minutes. Transfer with a slotted spoon to a bowl. Add the pasta to the same water and cook until al dente, about 10 minutes. Drain, reserving ¼ cup cooking water. Preheat the broiler.

3. Combine the egg mixture and the grated cheeses in the empty pot and cook over medium-low heat, stirring constantly, until the cheeses melt and the sauce begins to thicken. Remove from the heat and add the cauliflower. Puree with an immersion blender until smooth and light (you can also use a regular blender). Stir in some of the reserved cooking water until creamy.

4. Toss the pasta in the sauce; season with salt and black pepper. Transfer to a shallow casserole dish and top with the muenster slices. Broil until golden brown, about 5 minutes.

Per serving: Calories 403; Fat 17 g (Saturated 10 g); Cholesterol 85 mg; Sodium 517 mg; Carbohydrate 41 g; Fiber 2 g; Protein 20 g

Penne with Turkey Ragu

SERVES 4

ACTIVE: 25 min

TOTAL: 35 min

Kosher salt

1 tablespoon extra-virgin olive oil

2 leeks (white and light green parts only), finely chopped

2 cloves garlic, minced

6 ounces ground turkey

1 28-ounce can San Marzano tomatoes, crushed by hand

Freshly ground pepper

¼ cup fresh basil, chopped, plus more for topping

3 tablespoons freshly grated parmesan cheese, plus a small piece rind (optional)

12 ounces penne

2 tablespoons half-and-half

The secret ingredient in this meat sauce is half-and-half: Just 2 tablespoons give the sauce a rich flavor.

1. Bring a large pot of salted water to a boil. Meanwhile, heat the olive oil in a large skillet over medium heat. Add the leeks, garlic and turkey and cook, stirring, until the turkey browns slightly, about 5 minutes. Add the tomatoes, 2 cups water and ¼ teaspoon each salt and pepper. Increase the heat to high, bring the sauce to a boil and cook 5 minutes. Reduce the heat to medium, add half of the basil and the parmesan rind and simmer, stirring occasionally, until thickened, about 10 minutes.

2. Add the pasta to the boiling water and cook as the label directs. Reserve ½ cup of the cooking water, then drain the pasta. Stir the half-and-half, the remaining basil and 2 tablespoons cheese into the sauce. Add the pasta and toss to coat, adding some of the reserved cooking water to loosen, if needed. Remove the parmesan rind and season with salt and pepper.

3. Divide the pasta among bowls. Top with the remaining 1 tablespoon cheese and more basil.

Per serving: Calories 493; Fat 8 g (Saturated 3 g); Cholesterol 27 mg; Sodium 392 mg; Carbohydrate 79 g; Fiber 7 g; Protein 26 g

Chinese Noodle–Vegetable Bowl

Vegetarian | Vegan

SERVES 4

ACTIVE: 35 min
TOTAL: 40 min

Kosher salt

1 8-ounce package thin Chinese noodles

1 12-ounce package broccoli slaw

2 teaspoons toasted sesame oil

1 14-ounce package extra-firm tofu, drained and cut into ½-inch cubes

¼ cup vegetable oil

6 scallions, cut into 1-inch pieces

1 tablespoon minced peeled ginger

2 5-ounce packages sliced shiitake mushrooms

2 cups low-sodium mushroom or vegetable broth

2 tablespoons soy sauce

Freshly ground pepper

2 teaspoons cornstarch

Mushroom broth adds deep "meaty" flavor to these vegetarian noodles. To make your own, simmer 1½ cups mushroom stems in 3 to 4 cups water with a splash of soy sauce for about 25 minutes. Strain, then whisk in 1 tablespoon miso paste.

1. Bring a large pot of salted water to a boil. Add the noodles and broccoli slaw; cook, stirring, until the noodles are al dente and the slaw is tender, about 3 minutes. Drain and rinse under cold water, then transfer to a large bowl. Add the sesame oil, season with salt and toss.

2. Meanwhile, spread out the tofu on a kitchen towel; lay another towel on top and press to remove as much water as possible. Heat 2 tablespoons vegetable oil in a Dutch oven or large deep skillet over high heat. Add the tofu and cook, turning, until golden, about 6 minutes. Transfer to a paper towel–lined plate using a slotted spoon; season with salt.

3. Heat the remaining 2 tablespoons vegetable oil in the pot. Add the scallions and ginger; stir-fry 30 seconds. Add the shiitakes; stir-fry 3 minutes. Add the broth, soy sauce and tofu; season with pepper. Cook until the liquid is reduced by half, 3 to 4 minutes.

4. Whisk 3 tablespoons water and the cornstarch in a bowl; add to the pot and cook, stirring, until thickened. Add the noodles and toss to coat.

Per serving: Calories 466; Fat 25 g (Saturated 3 g); Cholesterol 41 mg; Sodium 560 mg; Carbohydrate 44 g; Fiber 8 g; Protein 23 g

Barley Risotto with Ham and Mushrooms

SERVES 4

ACTIVE: 40 min

TOTAL: 40 min

- 3 tablespoons unsalted butter
- 2 medium shallots, sliced
- 1½ cups quick-cooking barley
- 1 teaspoon fennel seeds (optional)
- Kosher salt and freshly ground pepper
- 10 ounces cremini or white button mushrooms, sliced
- ½ teaspoon minced fresh rosemary
- ½ cup dry white wine
- 2 cups low-sodium chicken broth
- 1 cup diced ham steak
- ½ cup grated parmesan cheese (about 1 ounce)
- ¼ cup chopped fresh parsley

Make barley one of your go-to grains: It's high in fiber and low on the glycemic index, which means it won't spike your blood sugar levels like some carbs can.

1. Melt the butter in a medium saucepan over medium-high heat. Add the shallots and cook until just soft, about 2 minutes. Add the barley, fennel seeds, ¼ teaspoon salt, and pepper to taste and cook, stirring, until the barley is lightly toasted, about 4 minutes. Add the mushrooms, rosemary and wine and cook, stirring, until the mushrooms are soft and the wine is absorbed, about 3 minutes.

2. Add the chicken broth and bring to a simmer; cover, reduce the heat to medium low and cook until the barley is tender and almost all of the liquid is absorbed, 8 to 10 minutes. Stir in the ham, parmesan and parsley. Season with salt and pepper.

Per serving: Calories 498; Fat 16 g (Saturated 9 g); Cholesterol 62 mg; Sodium 565 mg; Carbohydrate 64 g; Fiber 13 g; Protein 18 g

Ham and Black-Eyed Pea Salad

SERVES 4

ACTIVE: 10 min
TOTAL: 25 min

¾ cup quick-cooking barley

2 cups frozen black-eyed peas

3 tablespoons extra-virgin
   olive oil

3 tablespoons sherry vinegar
   or red wine vinegar

2 tablespoons light mayonnaise

   Kosher salt and freshly
   ground pepper

7 ounces mixed baby greens
   (about 12 cups)

¼ pound deli ham (preferably
   low sodium), in 1 piece,
   chopped

1½ cups cherry tomatoes, halved

5 radishes, chopped

4 scallions, chopped

2 tablespoons chopped dill
   pickles or cornichons

Keep an eye out for black-eyed peas in the freezer aisle: They have a nice firm texture, and they're not as salty as most of the canned ones.

1. Bring a medium pot of water to a boil. Add the barley, then reduce the heat to medium and simmer 7 minutes; add the black-eyed peas and continue cooking until both the barley and black-eyed peas are tender, about 5 more minutes. Drain and rinse under cold water.

2. Whisk the olive oil, vinegar, mayonnaise, ¼ teaspoon salt, and pepper to taste in a large bowl. Add the greens, ham, tomatoes, radishes, scallions, pickles, barley and black-eyed peas and toss. Divide among plates.

Per serving: Calories 376; Fat 15 g (Saturated 2 g); Cholesterol 15 mg; Sodium 472 mg; Carbohydrate 48 g; Fiber 9 g; Protein 16 g

Quinoa and Bean Pilaf

Vegetarian | Gluten-Free

SERVES 4

ACTIVE: 25 min

TOTAL: 40 min

- 2 tablespoons extra-virgin olive oil
- 2 bell peppers (1 red, 1 green), cut into ½-inch pieces
- 3 scallions, sliced (white and green parts separated)
- 2 stalks celery, diced
- 2 cloves garlic, finely chopped
- 2 tablespoons tomato paste
  Pinch of cayenne pepper
  Kosher salt
- 1 cup quinoa, well rinsed
- 2 15-ounce cans black and/or kidney beans, drained and rinsed
- 4 cups baby spinach (about 3 ounces)
- ½ cup shredded cheddar or pepper jack cheese
  Hot sauce, for serving (optional)

This is a great dish for vegetarians: Quinoa is considered a complete protein.

1. Heat the olive oil in a large skillet over medium-high heat. Add the bell peppers, scallion whites and celery and cook, stirring, until soft, about 5 minutes. Add the garlic, tomato paste, cayenne and ½ teaspoon salt and cook, stirring often, until the tomato paste turns brick red, about 2 minutes. Stir in the quinoa, then add 2 cups water and the beans. Bring to a simmer and cook, stirring often, until most of the water is absorbed and the quinoa is cooked through, about 15 minutes. Add up to ¼ cup more water if necessary.

2. Remove the skillet from the heat and stir in the spinach until just wilted. Stir in ½ teaspoon salt and half each of the scallion greens and cheese. Divide among bowls and sprinkle with the remaining scallion greens and cheese. Serve with hot sauce.

Per serving: Calories 394; Fat 15 g (Saturated 4 g); Cholesterol 15 mg; Sodium 724 mg; Carbohydrate 53 g; Fiber 9 g; Protein 16 g

SNACK TIME!

Try some new toppings on your crostini.

BEET-ORANGE
Spread toasted baguette with goat cheese; top with finely chopped cooked beets, an orange segment and fresh mint.

PESTO-PARMESAN
Top toasted baguette with pesto and shaved parmesan cheese.

APPLE–BLUE CHEESE
Spread toasted baguette with apple butter; top with crumbled blue cheese and chopped fresh sage.

ASPARAGUS-EGG

Halve asparagus tips lengthwise; steam until tender and season with salt; spread egg salad on toasted baguette; top with an asparagus tip.

FENNEL-RAISIN

Sauté thinly sliced fennel and golden raisins in olive oil until soft; spoon onto toasted baguette. Top with fennel fronds.

GRAPE-BACON

Spread toasted baguette with mascarpone; top with crumbled cooked bacon and chopped grapes.

FIG-HONEY

Top toasted baguette with sliced figs; drizzle with honey and sprinkle with sea salt.

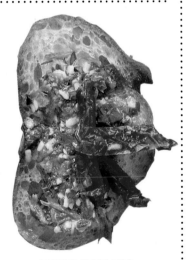

PESTO-TOMATO

Top toasted baguette with pesto and chopped sun-dried tomatoes.

BRIE-HAM

Spread toasted baguette with brie; top with thinly sliced ham and a dollop of grainy mustard.

SIDE DISHES

Bulgur Salad with Oranges and Olives

Vegetarian | Vegan

SERVES 4

ACTIVE: 10 min
TOTAL: 30 min

¾ cup bulgur wheat

1½ cups diced cucumber

⅓ cup chopped olives

¼ cup chopped fresh parsley

1 orange, cut into segments

¼ cup fresh orange juice

1 tablespoon extra-virgin olive oil

Kosher salt and freshly ground pepper

Bulgur wheat is high in fiber and makes for a filling side dish. It's a key ingredient in tabbouleh, the classic Middle Eastern salad.

1. Bring 1½ cups water to a boil. Add the bulgur and reduce the heat to medium. Cover and simmer until tender, about 20 minutes.

2. Meanwhile, combine the cucumber, olives, parsley and orange segments in a large bowl. Add the orange juice and olive oil and toss.

3. Rinse the cooked bulgur under cold water; add to the bowl and toss to combine. Season with salt and pepper.

Per serving: Calories 170; Fat 5 g (Saturated 1 g); Cholesterol 0 mg; Sodium 84 mg; Carbohydrate 29 g; Fiber 6 g; Protein 4 g

Tuscan White Beans

Vegetarian | Gluten-Free

SERVES 4

ACTIVE: 20 min

TOTAL: 20 min

 2 tablespoons olive oil, plus
 more for drizzling

 2 cloves garlic, smashed

 ¼ teaspoon red pepper flakes

 1 plum tomato, chopped

 1 sprig rosemary

 2 15-ounce cans cannellini
 beans, drained and rinsed

 ¼ cup chopped fresh parsley

 Kosher salt

 2 tablespoons grated parmesan
 cheese

Parmesan is an ideal cheese for low-fat cooking: It's super flavorful, so you need to use only a small amount.

1. Preheat the broiler. Heat the olive oil in a large ovenproof skillet over medium-high heat. Add the garlic and red pepper flakes and cook, stirring, until the garlic is slightly golden, about 1 minute. Add the tomato and rosemary sprig and cook until the tomato softens, about 2 minutes. Add the beans and cook, partially smashing the beans with a spoon, about 5 minutes. Remove the rosemary sprig.

2. Add ½ cup water to the skillet along with the parsley; season with salt and stir to combine. Sprinkle with the parmesan, transfer the skillet to the broiler and broil until golden. Drizzle with olive oil.

Per serving: Calories 248; Fat 10 g (Saturated 1 g); Cholesterol 3 mg; Sodium 131 mg; Carbohydrate 29 g; Fiber 9 g; Protein 12 g

Super-Stuffed Baked Potatoes

Gluten-Free

SERVES 4

ACTIVE: 30 min

TOTAL: 1 hr 30 min

- 2 slices bacon
- 4 russet potatoes (about 8 ounces each)
- 1 teaspoon extra-virgin olive oil
  Kosher salt and freshly ground pepper
- 3 cups cauliflower florets (from about 1 small head)
- 1/3 cup buttermilk
- 1 small clove garlic, grated
- 1 teaspoon white vinegar
- 1/8 teaspoon hot paprika, plus more for topping
- 1/2 cup shredded sharp cheddar cheese
- 2 scallions, thinly sliced

When you're making baked potatoes, brush with olive oil or melted butter first; it'll crisp the skin.

1. Cook the bacon in a skillet over medium heat, turning, until crisp, about 10 minutes. Transfer to paper towels to drain and reserve 1 tablespoon of the drippings. Chop the bacon.

2. Preheat the oven to 400°. Rub the potatoes with the olive oil and season with salt and pepper. Place on a baking sheet and bake 30 minutes. Pierce each potato in a few spots with a fork and continue baking until tender, 15 to 20 more minutes.

3. Meanwhile, fit a medium pot with a steamer basket, fill with 2 inches of water and bring to a boil. Add the cauliflower, cover and steam until crisp-tender, about 10 minutes. Transfer the cauliflower to a food processor. Add the buttermilk, garlic, vinegar, paprika, the reserved bacon drippings, 1/2 teaspoon salt, and pepper to taste; pulse until smooth.

4. Slice a thin layer off the top of each potato, then scoop the flesh into a bowl, leaving a 1/4-inch-thick wall. Mix the potato flesh with all but 1/4 cup of the cauliflower puree; mix in three-quarters each of the cheese and scallions, 1/2 teaspoon salt, and pepper to taste. Stuff the potato skins with the potato-cauliflower mixture and sprinkle with the remaining cheese. Bake until the cheese melts and the filling is warmed through, about 12 minutes. Top with the remaining cauliflower puree and scallions, the bacon and more paprika.

Per serving: Calories 290; Fat 7 g (Saturated 3 g); Cholesterol 20 mg; Sodium 703 mg; Carbohydrate 47 g; Fiber 5 g; Protein 12 g

Roasted Carrots with Raisins and Walnuts

Vegetarian | Vegan | Gluten-Free

SERVES 4

ACTIVE: 15 min

TOTAL: 35 min

- 8 carrots, cut into 1-inch sticks
- 1 red onion, chopped
- 1 tablespoon walnut oil
- ⅛ teaspoon ground allspice
  Kosher salt
- ¼ cup raisins
- ¼ cup walnuts, chopped
  Juice of 1 lemon
- 1 tablespoon chopped fresh cilantro
- 1 tablespoon chopped fresh dill

Carrots are high in vitamins A and K. If you're trying to get everyone in the family to eat more of them, try roasting: It concentrates the sweetness.

1. Preheat the oven to 425°. Toss the carrots with the red onion, walnut oil, allspice, and salt to taste on a baking sheet. Roast until just slightly tender, about 10 minutes. Meanwhile, soak the raisins in ¼ cup water, 10 minutes.

2. Drain the raisins and add to the carrots along with the walnuts. Stir and continue roasting until the carrots are golden, about 10 more minutes. Toss with the lemon juice, cilantro and dill and season with salt.

Per serving: **Calories** 176; **Fat** 9 g (Saturated 1 g); **Cholesterol** 0 mg; **Sodium** 88 mg; **Carbohydrate** 24 g; **Fiber** 5 g; **Protein** 3 g

Kale and Pear Salad

Vegetarian | Vegan | Gluten-Free

SERVES 4

ACTIVE: 15 min

TOTAL: 15 min

- ½ large bunch kale, leaves chopped
- ¼ cup extra-virgin olive oil
- 3 tablespoons white wine vinegar

  Kosher salt
- ½ cup chopped pecans
- ¼ teaspoon sugar
- 1 pear, chopped

  Freshly ground pepper

Hearty greens like kale, chard and collards are delicious in salads, but they can be tough. To soften them, toss the leaves with a little oil and vinegar, then rub with your fingers until slightly wilted.

1. Toss the kale with 1 tablespoon each olive oil and vinegar and ¼ teaspoon salt in a large bowl; rub with your fingers until softened and slightly wilted.

2. Combine 1 tablespoon olive oil, the pecans, sugar and ¼ teaspoon salt in a large skillet over medium heat; cook, stirring, until the nuts are toasted. Stir in the chopped pear.

3. Add the pecan-pear mixture to the bowl with the kale. Drizzle with the remaining 2 tablespoons each olive oil and vinegar, season with salt and pepper and toss.

Per serving: Calories 268; Fat 25 g (Saturated 3 g); Cholesterol 0 mg; Sodium 133 mg; Carbohydrate 12 g; Fiber 3 g; Protein 2 g

Artichoke and Pea Gratin

Vegetarian

SERVES 4

ACTIVE: 15 min

TOTAL: 20 min

1 tablespoon unsalted butter

1 tablespoon all-purpose flour

1¼ cups low-fat milk

1 9-ounce package frozen artichoke hearts, thawed

1 cup frozen peas, thawed

½ teaspoon grated lemon zest

Kosher salt

Grated parmesan cheese, for topping

Try cooking with frozen artichokes: They don't contain any of the salty brine, oil or tough outer leaves that you often find in canned and jarred artichokes.

1. Preheat the broiler. Melt the butter in a medium ovenproof skillet over medium-high heat; whisk in the flour and cook, whisking, 1 minute. Whisk in the milk until smooth; bring to a boil, whisking.

2. Add the artichokes, peas, lemon zest and ½ teaspoon salt to the skillet and stir to combine. Bring to a simmer. Sprinkle with parmesan, transfer the skillet to the broiler and broil until golden.

Per serving: Calories 155; Fat 5 g (Saturated 3 g); Cholesterol 16 mg; Sodium 296 mg; Carbohydrate 17 g; Fiber 3 g; Protein 9 g

Warm Beet-Orange Salad

Vegetarian | Vegan | Gluten-Free

SERVES 4

ACTIVE: 15 min
TOTAL: 1 hr 5 min

- 1 pound beets, trimmed
- 3 tablespoons extra-virgin olive oil
- ⅓ cup fresh orange juice
  Kosher salt
- 2 oranges, cut into segments
- ¼ cup walnuts, toasted and chopped

Roasted beets are super easy to peel. Just wrap in foil, roast as directed and let cool slightly before opening. You should be able to rub off the skin with a paper towel.

1. Preheat the oven to 400°. Place the beets on a large piece of foil. Drizzle with 1 tablespoon olive oil and 3 tablespoons water; close into a packet. Transfer to the oven and roast until tender, about 50 minutes. Let cool slightly before opening.

2. Peel the beets and cut into wedges. Whisk the orange juice, the remaining 2 tablespoons olive oil, and salt to taste in a bowl. Add the beets, orange segments and walnuts and gently toss.

Per serving: Calories 244; Fat 16 g (Saturated 2 g); Cholesterol 0 mg; Sodium 84 mg; Carbohydrate 25 g; Fiber 5 g; Protein 4 g

Texas Black-Eyed Peas

Gluten-Free

SERVES 4

ACTIVE: 20 min

TOTAL: 20 min

- 3 slices thick-cut bacon, chopped
- 1 cup celery, sliced
- 4 scallions, chopped
- ¾ teaspoon chili powder
  Kosher salt
- 1 1-pound package frozen black-eyed peas
  Chopped parsley, for topping

Bacon is much easier to chop when it's cold. Keep a stash in the freezer for weeknight meals and dice it frozen.

1. Cook the bacon in a skillet over medium-high heat until crisp, about 6 minutes. Add the celery, scallions, chili powder and ½ teaspoon salt. Cook, stirring, until the celery is translucent, about 4 minutes.

2. Add the frozen black-eyed peas and ¾ cup water. Reduce the heat to medium and cook until warmed through, about 5 minutes. Transfer to a bowl and top with parsley.

Per serving: Calories 260; Fat 9 g (Saturated 3 g); Cholesterol 10 mg; Sodium 440 mg; Carbohydrate 33 g; Fiber 8 g; Protein 14 g

Carrot and Parsnip Fries

Vegetarian

SERVES 4

ACTIVE: 15 min

TOTAL: 50 min

1 pound carrots

1 pound parsnips

1 tablespoon vegetable oil

1 teaspoon lemon-pepper seasoning

Kosher salt

2 large egg whites, lightly beaten

½ cup panko breadcrumbs

Large parsnips have a fibrous core running through the middle. To remove it, quarter the parsnips lengthwise, then slice off the core.

1. Preheat the oven to 400°. Cut the carrots and parsnips into ½-inch-thick sticks. Toss with the vegetable oil, lemon-pepper seasoning and 1 teaspoon salt in a bowl. Add the egg whites and toss, then add the panko and toss to coat.

2. Spread the fries on 2 baking sheets. Transfer to the oven and bake, stirring once, until crisp, about 35 minutes.

Per serving: Calories 198; Fat 4 g (Saturated 1 g); Cholesterol 0 mg; Sodium 701 mg; Carbohydrate 37 g; Fiber 9 g; Protein 5 g

Broccoli with Walnut Romesco Sauce

Vegetarian | Vegan | Gluten-Free

SERVES 4

ACTIVE: 20 min
TOTAL: 20 min

¼ cup extra-virgin olive oil

2 cloves garlic

½ large roasted red pepper
(about 3 ounces)

½ cup walnuts

1 tablespoon tomato paste

1 tablespoon sherry vinegar

2 teaspoons smoked paprika

Kosher salt

¼ teaspoon ancho chile powder

1 head broccoli

Traditional Spanish Romesco sauce is made with almonds, but we used walnuts for this version. Make a double batch and serve it as a topping for chicken or fish.

1. Heat the olive oil in a skillet over medium heat. Add the whole garlic cloves and cook until golden, about 3 minutes. Transfer to a blender or food processor and add the roasted red pepper, walnuts, 2 tablespoons water, the tomato paste, vinegar, paprika, ½ teaspoon salt and the chile powder. Pulse until smooth; set aside.

2. Fit a saucepan with a steamer basket, fill with 2 inches of water and bring to a simmer. Add the broccoli, cover and steam until crisp-tender, 3 to 5 minutes. Serve the steamed broccoli with the Romesco sauce.

Per serving: Calories 311; Fat 24 g (Saturated 3 g); Cholesterol 0 mg; Sodium 506 mg; Carbohydrate 18 g; Fiber 6 g; Protein 8 g

Garden Potato Salad with Yogurt Dressing

Vegetarian | Gluten-Free

SERVES 6 to 8

ACTIVE: 25 min

TOTAL: 35 min (plus chilling)

Potato cooking water is just like pasta water: It's starchy and flavorful and can help a sauce or dressing come together, so remember to reserve some.

1 lemon

5 sprigs parsley, plus
  2 tablespoons chopped
  leaves

2 sprigs thyme

1 bay leaf

3 cloves garlic, smashed

2 pounds small red-skinned
  potatoes, sliced ¼ inch thick

  Kosher salt

4 medium carrots, sliced
  ¼ inch thick

¾ cup fat-free plain yogurt

¼ cup low-fat mayonnaise

1 tablespoon plus 1 teaspoon
  whole-grain or dijon mustard

3 scallions, minced (white and
  green parts separated)

  Freshly ground pepper

2 stalks celery, sliced
  ¼ inch thick

1 small Kirby cucumber,
  sliced ¼ inch thick

1. Peel a 2-inch-long strip of zest from the lemon; tie into a bundle with the parsley and thyme sprigs and bay leaf using kitchen twine. Put in a saucepan with the garlic, potatoes, 2 tablespoons salt and 8 cups water. Bring to a boil, then reduce to a simmer and cook about 10 minutes. Add the carrots and cook until the potatoes are tender and the carrots are crisp-tender, about 5 more minutes. Reserve ¼ cup of the cooking water, then drain the vegetables and discard the herb bundle. Let cool.

2. Meanwhile, finely grate 2 teaspoons lemon zest and squeeze 3 tablespoons juice into a large bowl. Whisk in the yogurt, mayonnaise, mustard, scallion whites, chopped parsley, reserved cooking water, 1 teaspoon salt and ¾ teaspoon pepper.

3. Add the potatoes, carrots, celery and cucumber to the dressing and toss. Cover and refrigerate about 4 hours. Top with the scallion greens.

Per serving: Calories 175; Fat 4 g (Saturated 1 g); Cholesterol 4 mg; Sodium 712 mg; Carbohydrate 30 g; Fiber 5 g; Protein 6 g

Low-Fat Scalloped Potatoes
Vegetarian

SERVES 6 to 8

ACTIVE: 15 min
TOTAL: 40 min

2 tablespoons unsalted butter, plus more for the dish

Kosher salt

3 pounds Yukon gold potatoes, peeled and thinly sliced

2 tablespoons all-purpose flour

1 cup low-fat (1%) milk, at room temperature

1 cup whole milk, at room temperature

Freshly ground pepper

¼ teaspoon freshly grated nutmeg

¼ cup grated gruyère cheese

We used a combination of low-fat and full-fat milk in this dish: A little fat helps stabilize the milk and keeps it from curdling in the oven.

1. Preheat the oven to 350°. Lightly butter a 3-quart baking dish. Bring a large pot of salted water to a boil; add the potatoes and cook until just tender, 8 to 10 minutes. Drain the potatoes and return to the pot.

2. Meanwhile, melt 2 tablespoons butter in a saucepan over medium heat. Stir in the flour with a wooden spoon to make a paste. Cook, stirring, until the paste puffs slightly, about 1 minute. Gradually whisk in both milks and simmer, whisking constantly, until thickened, about 3 minutes. Remove from the heat and whisk in ½ teaspoon pepper, 1½ teaspoons salt and the nutmeg. Pour the sauce over the potatoes and gently toss to coat.

3. Transfer the potato mixture to the prepared baking dish and sprinkle with the gruyère. Bake until heated through, about 10 minutes. Turn on the broiler and broil the potatoes until browned on top, about 5 minutes. Let rest 10 minutes before serving.

Per serving: Calories 290; Fat 7 g (Saturated 4 g); Cholesterol 22 mg; Sodium 546 mg; Carbohydrate 46 g; Fiber 3 g; Protein 10 g

Tropical Watercress Salad

Vegetarian | Vegan | Gluten-Free

SERVES 4

ACTIVE: 15 min

TOTAL: 15 min

- ½ small red onion, thinly sliced
- ¼ cup extra-virgin olive oil
  Juice of 1 lime
  Juice of ½ orange
- 1 15-ounce can hearts of palm, rinsed, drained and sliced
- 1 mango, thinly sliced
- 1 jalapeño pepper, thinly sliced (remove seeds for less heat)
- 1 bunch watercress, trimmed and torn
  Kosher salt

The entire watercress plant is edible, but the stems at the base can be tough: Trim off the bottom inch or two before using.

1. Soak the red onion slices in a bowl of ice water, 10 minutes.

2. Whisk the olive oil with the lime juice and orange juice in a large bowl. Add the hearts of palm, mango and jalapeño. Drain the onion and add to the bowl along with the watercress. Season with salt and toss.

Per serving: Calories 207; Fat 15 g (Saturated 2 g); Cholesterol 0 mg; Sodium 457 mg; Carbohydrate 18 g; Fiber 4 g; Protein 3 g

Pickled Strawberry Salad

Vegetarian | Gluten-Free

SERVES 4

ACTIVE: 15 min

TOTAL: 25 min

2 cups strawberries,
hulled and halved

1 shallot, thinly sliced

3 tablespoons sherry vinegar

2 teaspoons sugar

Kosher salt

2 tablespoons extra-virgin
olive oil

1 teaspoon dijon mustard

Freshly ground pepper

6 cups mesclun greens

2 tablespoons hazelnuts,
toasted and chopped

2 ounces goat cheese,
crumbled

Pickling isn't just for veggies! We made quick strawberry pickles for this salad, but you could use the same formula with other relatively firm fruit, including grapes, peaches, plums and cherries.

1. Toss the strawberries and shallot in a large bowl with the vinegar, sugar and a pinch of salt; let sit 10 minutes. Remove the berries and shallot with a slotted spoon and set aside.

2. Whisk the olive oil, mustard, and a pinch each of salt and pepper into the vinegar mixture. Add the greens and the strawberry mixture. Top with the hazelnuts and goat cheese.

Per serving: Calories 187; Fat 12 g (Saturated 3 g); Cholesterol 7 mg; Sodium 219 mg; Carbohydrate 17 g; Fiber 4 g; Protein 6 g

Quinoa-Tomato Salad

Vegetarian | Vegan | Gluten-Free

SERVES 4

ACTIVE: 20 min

TOTAL: 30 min

Kosher salt

1 cup quinoa, well rinsed

1 cup grape tomatoes, halved

1 15-ounce can hearts of palm, drained, rinsed and sliced

2 scallions, chopped

2 tablespoons extra-virgin olive oil

Pinch of sugar

Chopped fresh parsley, for topping

Be sure to rinse your quinoa well before cooking; the natural coating can taste a little bitter.

1. Bring 1½ cups salted water to a boil in a saucepan. Add the quinoa and reduce the heat to low; cover and simmer until tender, about 15 minutes. Stir to cool slightly.

2. Transfer the quinoa to a large bowl. Add the tomatoes, hearts of palm, scallions, olive oil and sugar and toss. Season with salt and top with parsley.

Per serving: Calories 264; Fat 10 g (Saturated 1 g); Cholesterol 0 mg; Sodium 468 mg; Carbohydrate 36 g; Fiber 5 g; Protein 9 g

Sesame-Ginger Snap Peas

Vegetarian | Vegan | Gluten-Free

SERVES 4

ACTIVE: 15 min

TOTAL: 15 min

1 pound sugar snap peas, strings removed

1 tablespoon minced shallot

2 teaspoons sherry vinegar

2 teaspoons toasted sesame oil

1 teaspoon grated peeled ginger

Kosher salt

Snap peas have tough strings on both sides of the pod. To remove them, pinch off the stem and pull the string, then repeat on the other end.

1. Fit a saucepan with a steamer basket and fill with 2 inches of water. Bring to a boil; add the snap peas, cover and cook until tender, about 3 minutes.

2. Transfer the snap peas to a bowl; add the shallot, vinegar, sesame oil, ginger and 1 teaspoon salt and toss.

Per serving: Calories 79; Fat 2 g (Saturated 0 g); Cholesterol 0 mg; Sodium 493 mg; Carbohydrate 11 g; Fiber 3 g; Protein 3 g

Corn on the Cob with Basil Butter

Vegetarian | Gluten-Free

SERVES 4

ACTIVE: 15 min

TOTAL: 15 min

4 tablespoons unsalted butter, softened

¼ cup fresh basil

Grated zest of 1 lemon

1 clove garlic

Kosher salt

4 ears of corn, husked

3 tablespoons shredded parmesan cheese

Freshly ground pepper

If you have extra herbs on hand, turn them into flavored butter: You can use any herbs in place of the basil in this recipe. Form the finished butter into a log using parchment paper, twist the ends and store in the fridge for up to 2 weeks.

1. Combine the butter, basil, lemon zest, garlic and a pinch of salt in a food processor and puree until smooth.

2. Bring a large pot of salted water to a boil. Add the corn and cook until tender, about 4 minutes. Drain, then top with the basil butter and parmesan; season with salt and pepper.

Per serving: Calories 202; Fat 14 g (Saturated 8 g); Cholesterol 34 mg; Sodium 227 mg; Carbohydrate 18 g; Fiber 3 g; Protein 5 g

SNACK TIME!

Put a new spin on popcorn—the ultimate low-cal snack.

TEQUILA-LIME POPCORN
Melt 6 tablespoons butter with
2 tablespoons each lime juice and
tequila, 2 teaspoons each sugar
and kosher salt, and 1½ teaspoons
grated lime zest; drizzle over
12 cups hot popcorn and toss
with 4 cups lightly crushed
lime-favored tortilla chips.

THREE-CHEESE POPCORN
Toss 16 cups hot popcorn with
2 cups shredded cheddar,
1 cup grated parmesan and ½ cup
grated pecorino; spread on baking
sheets. Bake at 350° until the
cheddar melts, 3 minutes.
Season with salt.

RANCH POPCORN
Melt 4 tablespoons butter with a
1-ounce packet ranch seasoning mix;
toss with 16 cups hot popcorn and
2 tablespoons chopped chives.
Season with salt.

CRAB BOIL POPCORN
Melt 4 tablespoons butter with
2 tablespoons Old Bay Seasoning;
drizzle over 12 cups hot popcorn and
toss with 4 cups oyster crackers.

TROPICAL POPCORN
Toss 16 cups hot popcorn with
2 cups toasted coconut,
1½ cups chopped dried pineapple
and 3 tablespoons each
confectioners' sugar and melted
butter. Season with salt.

SWEETS

Low-Fat Cheesecake

Vegetarian

SERVES 14

ACTIVE: 30 min

TOTAL: 2 hr 10 min (plus chilling)

- 9 low-fat cinnamon graham cracker sheets, broken in half
- 2 tablespoons unsalted butter, melted

Cooking spray

- 2 8-ounce packages Neufchâtel cream cheese, softened
- 2 8-ounce packages fat-free cream cheese, softened
- 1½ cups sugar, plus a pinch
- 1 cup reduced-fat sour cream
- 2 large eggs, plus 3 egg whites
- 2 tablespoons all-purpose flour
- 1 teaspoon pure vanilla extract
- 1 teaspoon finely grated lemon zest
- 1 cup sliced strawberries

Juice of 1 lemon

Overbaking can cause a cheesecake to crack. The cake is done when the middle 2 or 3 inches are still wobbly; the center will firm up as it cools.

1. Preheat the oven to 350°. Pulse the graham crackers in a food processor until ground. Add 1 to 2 tablespoons water and the butter; pulse until moistened. Wrap the outside of a 9-inch springform pan with foil to prevent leaks. Coat the inside of the pan with cooking spray and press the graham cracker crumbs onto the bottom. Bake until browned, about 8 minutes. Let cool, about 10 minutes.

2. Meanwhile, beat both cream cheeses and 1½ cups sugar with a mixer on medium-high speed until smooth, 5 minutes, then beat in the sour cream on low. Lightly whisk the 3 egg whites in a bowl, then add to the cream cheese mixture along with the 2 whole eggs, flour, vanilla and lemon zest. Beat on medium speed until fluffy, about 3 minutes. Pour over the crust.

3. Place the cheesecake in a roasting pan and add enough warm water to come one-quarter of the way up the sides of the springform. Bake until the cake is set around the edge but the center still jiggles, about 1 hour, 10 minutes. Turn off the oven; keep the cheesecake inside with the door closed for 20 minutes.

4. Remove the cake from the water bath and transfer to a rack. Run a knife around the edge, then cool completely. Chill until firm, at least 8 hours. Before serving, toss the strawberries with the lemon juice and a pinch of suger; let macerate 30 minutes. Serve with the cheesecake.

Per serving: **Calories** 229; **Fat** 11 g (Saturated 7 g); **Cholesterol** 61 mg; **Sodium** 319 mg; **Carbohydrate** 24 g; **Fiber** 0 g; **Protein** 11 g

Raspberry Corn Muffins

Vegetarian

MAKES 12 muffins

ACTIVE: 30 min
TOTAL: 1 hr

Cooking spray
1½ cups all-purpose flour
2½ cups yellow cornmeal
1½ cups sugar
1 tablespoon baking powder
¾ teaspoon salt
2 cups buttermilk
½ cup no-sugar-added apricot nectar
3 tablespoons grapeseed oil
2 teaspoons pure vanilla extract
1 teaspoon grated orange zest
4 large egg whites
2 cups frozen raspberries

Apricot nectar keeps these muffins moist and sweet without adding fat.

1. Preheat the oven to 375°. Line a 12-cup muffin pan with paper liners.

2. Whisk the flour, cornmeal, ¾ cup sugar, the baking powder and salt in a medium bowl. In another bowl, whisk the buttermilk, apricot nectar, grapeseed oil, vanilla extract and orange zest until combined.

3. Beat the egg whites and the remaining ¾ cup sugar in a large bowl with a mixer on medium-high speed until stiff peaks form, about 8 minutes. Whisk the buttermilk mixture into the dry ingredients until just moistened. Gently fold in the egg-white mixture until almost combined, then fold in the raspberries; do not overmix.

4. Divide the batter among the prepared muffin cups (an ice cream scoop works well). Bake until a toothpick inserted into a muffin comes out clean, 30 to 35 minutes. Remove the muffins from the pan and let cool on a rack.

Per muffin: Calories 293; Fat 5 g (Saturated 1 g); Cholesterol 3 mg; Sodium 338 mg; Carbohydrate 60 g; Fiber 3 g; Protein 7 g

Melon–Green Tea Slushies

Vegetarian | Vegan | Gluten-Free

MAKES 4 drinks

ACTIVE: 15 min

TOTAL: 15 min (plus 2-hr freezing)

- 2 bags green tea
- 2 tablespoons sugar
- 1 1-inch piece ginger, peeled and thinly sliced
- 3 cups chopped honeydew melon
- 1 12-ounce can ginger ale
- ¼ cup fresh lemon juice
- ¼ cup fresh mint

Green tea can taste bitter, but it's great in these slushies. Bonus: It's super high in antioxidants.

1. Bring 1½ cups water to a simmer in a medium saucepan. Remove from the heat, add the tea bags and let steep 5 minutes. Remove the tea bags (do not squeeze). Let the tea cool to room temperature.

2. Meanwhile, bring 3 tablespoons water, the sugar and ginger to a simmer in a small saucepan over medium heat; cook, stirring, until the sugar dissolves, about 2 minutes. Remove from the heat and let cool. Strain the syrup into the tea and discard the ginger. Pour into ice cube trays and freeze until solid, 2 to 4 hours. Freeze the chopped melon until solid, at least 2 hours.

3. Combine half each of the tea ice cubes, frozen melon, ginger ale, lemon juice and mint in a blender and puree until smooth. Divide between 2 glasses. Repeat to make 2 more drinks.

Per serving: **Calories** 95; **Fat** 0 g (**Saturated** 0 g); **Cholesterol** 0 mg; **Sodium** 34 mg; **Carbohydrate** 26 g; **Fiber** 1 g; **Protein** 1 g

Oatmeal-Flax Chocolate Chip Cookies

Vegetarian

MAKES about 32 cookies

ACTIVE: 35 min

TOTAL: 1 hr

- 1½ cups all-purpose flour
- 1 cup quick-cooking oats
- ¼ cup flaxseeds, finely ground (or pre-ground flaxseeds)
- 1 teaspoon baking soda
- ½ teaspoon salt
- ½ teaspoon ground cinnamon
- 12 tablespoons (1½ sticks) unsalted butter, at room temperature
- 1 cup granulated sugar
- ¾ cup packed dark brown sugar
- 2 large eggs
- 1 teaspoon pure vanilla extract
- 1 cup semisweet chocolate chips

Flaxseeds are loaded with protein, essential fatty acids and fiber. Grind them in a spice grinder before using—your body will absorb the nutrients more easily.

1. Preheat the oven to 350°. Line 2 baking sheets with parchment paper.

2. Whisk the flour, oats, flaxseeds, baking soda, salt and cinnamon in a bowl.

3. Beat the butter, granulated sugar and brown sugar in a large bowl with a mixer on medium-high speed until fluffy, about 4 minutes. Beat in the eggs one at a time, beating well after each addition. Beat in the vanilla. Reduce the mixer speed to low; add the flour mixture and beat until just combined, scraping down the bowl as needed. Stir in the chocolate chips.

4. Drop heaping tablespoonfuls of dough onto the prepared baking sheets, about 2 inches apart. Bake until golden brown, 10 to 12 minutes. Let the cookies cool 3 minutes on the baking sheets, then transfer to racks to cool completely.

Per cookie: **Calories** 144; **Fat** 7 g (Saturated 4 g); **Cholesterol** 25 mg; **Sodium** 75 mg; **Carbohydrate** 21 g; **Fiber** 1 g; **Protein** 2 g

Low-Fat Chocolate Pudding

Vegetarian | Gluten-Free

SERVES 6

ACTIVE: 30 min

TOTAL: 30 min (plus chilling)

- ⅓ cup agave nectar or packed light brown sugar
- 2 tablespoons cornstarch
  Pinch of salt
- 2 12-ounce cans fat-free evaporated milk
- 2 large egg whites, lightly beaten
- 1 tablespoon plus 1 teaspoon pure vanilla extract
- 2 tablespoons white chocolate chips
- ¼ cup unsweetened cocoa powder
- 2 tablespoons semisweet chocolate chips

Classic pudding calls for whole milk; we used fat-free evaporated milk instead and saved about 3 grams of fat per serving.

1. Whisk the agave nectar, cornstarch and salt in a heavy-bottomed pot. Whisk in the evaporated milk and egg whites until well combined. Cook over medium-low heat, whisking constantly, until the mixture bubbles and thickens, about 10 minutes. Remove from the heat; stir in 1 tablespoon vanilla.

2. Transfer 1 cup of the mixture to a medium bowl. Add the white chocolate chips and the remaining 1 teaspoon vanilla and stir until the chips melt. Add the cocoa powder and semisweet chocolate chips to the remaining pudding and stir until the chips melt.

3. Divide the chocolate pudding among dishes and top with the vanilla pudding. Cover with plastic wrap and refrigerate until set, at least 2 hours.

Per serving: **Calories** 228; **Fat** 3 g (**Saturated** 2 g); **Cholesterol** 2 mg; **Sodium** 214 mg; **Carbohydrate** 38 g; **Fiber** 1 g; **Protein** 10 g

Strawberry Corn Cakes

Vegetarian

MAKES 6

ACTIVE: 25 min

TOTAL: 30 min (plus cooling)

Cooking spray

1 8.5-ounce box corn muffin mix

¼ cup all-purpose flour

2 teaspoons finely grated lemon zest

1 teaspoon pure vanilla extract

1 cup chopped strawberries

2 tablespoons strawberry preserves

¾ cup heavy cream

2 tablespoons confectioners' sugar

These berry-filled treats are incredibly easy: The base is just a box of store-bought corn muffin mix. With a little whipped cream on the side, they taste like strawberry shortcake.

1. Preheat the oven to 375°. Lightly coat a 6-cup muffin pan with cooking spray. Prepare the corn muffin batter as the label directs, then stir in the flour, lemon zest and vanilla.

2. Divide the batter evenly among the muffin cups. Bake until the edges are set and the centers are soft but not wet, 10 to 12 minutes. Meanwhile, toss the strawberries and strawberry preserves in a bowl and set aside.

3. Remove the corn cakes from the oven. Gently press the back of a teaspoon into the center of each to make an indentation about one-third of the way into the cake. Spoon about 2 teaspoons of the strawberry mixture into each indentation, pressing to tightly fill. (Reserve the remaining berry mixture for topping.) Return the cakes to the oven and continue baking until just golden, about 5 more minutes.

4. Let the cakes cool in the pan on a rack 5 minutes, then remove from the pan and let cool 10 more minutes. Meanwhile, beat the heavy cream and confectioners' sugar with a mixer until soft peaks form. Top the cakes with the remaining berry mixture and serve with the whipped cream.

Per serving: **Calories** 330; **Fat** 17 g (**Saturated** 10 g); **Cholesterol** 57 mg; **Sodium** 298 mg; **Carbohydrate** 42 g; **Fiber** 1 g; **Protein** 4 g

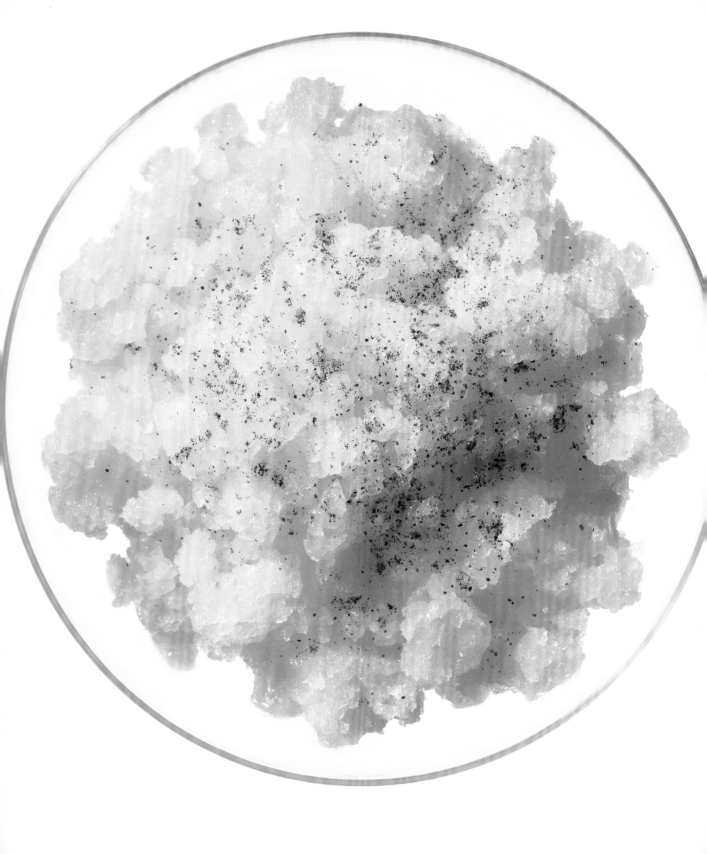

Mango-Chile Granita

Vegetarian | Vegan | Gluten-Free

SERVES 4

ACTIVE: 15 min

TOTAL: 25 min (plus 4-hr freezing)

- ¾ cup sugar
- 2 cups mango nectar
- 1 ripe mango,
  peeled and cubed
- Juice of 2 limes
- Kosher salt
- Ancho chile powder,
  for topping

Avoid using aluminum pans when you're making granita—the aluminum can react with the acidic ingredients and produce a metallic taste. Use stainless steel or glass instead.

1. Combine the sugar and ½ cup water in a medium saucepan and bring to a simmer over medium-high heat. Cook, stirring occasionally, until the sugar dissolves, about 1 minute; transfer to a blender and let cool completely.

2. Add the mango nectar, cubed mango, lime juice and a pinch of salt to the blender and puree until smooth. Press through a fine-mesh sieve into an 8-inch-square stainless-steel or glass baking dish.

3. Freeze until ice crystals begin forming around the edges, about 45 minutes. Use a fork to scrape the crystals toward the center of the pan, then continue freezing, scraping every 30 minutes, until frozen, about 4 hours. Serve topped with chile powder.

Per serving: **Calories** 187; **Fat** 0 g (**Saturated** 0 g); **Cholesterol** 0 mg; **Sodium** 66 mg; **Carbohydrate** 51 g; **Fiber** 1 g; **Protein** 0 g

Sweet Tofu-Raspberry Strudel

Vegetarian

SERVES 6 to 8

ACTIVE: 30 min

TOTAL: 50 min (plus cooling)

- 6 ounces firm silken tofu, at room temperature
- 1½ cups confectioners' sugar, plus more for dusting
- 3 ounces cream cheese, at room temperature
- 2 tablespoons all-purpose flour
- 1½ teaspoons pure vanilla extract
- 5 sheets frozen phyllo dough, thawed
- 6 tablespoons unsalted butter, melted
- 6 tablespoons graham cracker crumbs
- 1 cup raspberries

We pureed tofu to make this strudel. The "silken" kind works best; it's much softer and creamier than regular tofu.

1. Preheat the oven to 425°. Blend the tofu in a food processor until smooth. Add the confectioners' sugar, cream cheese, flour and vanilla and puree until combined.

2. Stack the phyllo sheets on a flat surface and cover with a slightly damp kitchen towel. Cut a piece of parchment paper slightly longer than the phyllo. Lay 1 sheet phyllo on the parchment with a long side facing you (keep the remaining phyllo covered). Brush with 1 tablespoon butter and sprinkle with 1 tablespoon graham cracker crumbs. Top with another sheet of phyllo, then more butter and crumbs. Repeat with the remaining phyllo sheets, topping each with butter and crumbs. Reserve the remaining butter and crumbs for topping.

3. Spoon the tofu mixture across the length of the phyllo, leaving a 1-inch border at the long edge closest to you and a 2-inch border at the short ends. Sprinkle the raspberries on top of the tofu mixture. Starting with the long edge, use the parchment to roll the phyllo tightly over the filling to make a log; turn seam-side down on the parchment. Brush with the remaining butter and sprinkle with the remaining crumbs.

4. Transfer the parchment and strudel to a baking sheet. Bake until golden, about 18 minutes, rotating the baking sheet halfway through. Slide the strudel onto a cutting board and let cool completely, about 1 hour. Dust with confectioners' sugar.

Per serving: **Calories** 356; **Fat** 18 g (Saturated 10 g); **Cholesterol** 46 mg; **Sodium** 136 mg; **Carbohydrate** 45 g; **Fiber** 1 g; **Protein** 5 g

Banana-Almond Pudding
Vegetarian

SERVES 4

ACTIVE: 20 min

TOTAL: 35 min (plus chilling)

- 1 cup reduced fat (2%) milk
- 1 cup plain unsweetened almond milk
- 3 tablespoons cornstarch
- Pinch of kosher salt
- ⅓ cup sugar
- 1 large egg
- 1 teaspoon pure vanilla extract
- 2 large bananas
- 6 low-fat cinnamon graham cracker sheets, broken into 1-inch pieces
- 1 tablespoon cocoa powder (sweetened or unsweetened)
- ¼ cup sliced almonds, toasted

Give almond milk a try: It has less than half the calories of skim milk, and it gives this pudding a subtle nutty flavor. Just be sure it's unsweetened.

1. Heat the milk and almond milk in a saucepan over medium heat until almost simmering; remove from the heat. Meanwhile, whisk the cornstarch, salt, sugar and egg in a medium heatproof bowl. Pour about half of the hot milk mixture into the bowl and whisk vigorously until smooth. Pour the mixture back into the saucepan and cook over medium heat, whisking vigorously, until thick and starting to bubble, 1 to 2 minutes. Whisk in the vanilla. Transfer the mixture to a bowl and let cool, stirring occasionally.

2. Thinly slice the bananas. Layer a few banana slices, a few pieces of graham cracker and 2 tablespoons of the prepared pudding in each of 4 glasses; sprinkle with cocoa powder and almonds, then repeat to make 2 more layers. Cover with plastic wrap and chill 4 hours or overnight.

Per serving: **Calories** 253; **Fat** 7 g (Saturated 2 g); **Cholesterol** 59 mg; **Sodium** 173 mg; **Carbohydrate** 45 g; **Fiber** 3 g; **Protein** 6 g

Coconut Macaroons

Vegetarian | Gluten-Free

MAKES about 30 cookies

ACTIVE: 10 min

TOTAL: 30 min (plus cooling)

  3 large egg whites
 ½ cup sugar
 ⅛ teaspoon salt
 ½ teaspoon pure vanilla extract
  1 14-ounce package sweetened
    shredded coconut

Macaroons are surprisingly low-fat: They're made without butter! For a chocolate version, whisk 2 tablespoons unsweetened cocoa powder into the egg white mixture before adding the coconut.

1. Preheat the oven to 325° and line a baking sheet with parchment paper. Whisk the egg whites, sugar, salt and vanilla in a large bowl until combined; fold in the coconut.

2. Scoop heaping tablespoonfuls of the coconut mixture about 1 inch apart onto the prepared baking sheet. Use your fingers to form into pyramids. Bake until golden brown around the edges, 20 to 25 minutes. Let cool 10 minutes on the baking sheet, then transfer to a rack to cool completely.

Per cookie: **Calories** 72; **Fat** 4 g (Saturated 4 g); **Cholesterol** 0 mg; **Sodium** 49 mg; **Carbohydrate** 8 g; **Fiber** 1 g; **Protein** 1 g

Hot Peaches and Cream

Vegetarian | Gluten-Free

SERVES 4

ACTIVE: 15 min

TOTAL: 15 min

- 4 peaches
- ⅓ cup elderflower liqueur (such as St-Germain) or sweet dessert wine
- 1 tablespoon unsalted butter
- 2 tablespoons plus 2 teaspoons demerara sugar
- ¼ cup mascarpone cheese or sour cream

This recipe is a simple way to showcase ripe stone fruit. You can use plums or nectarines instead of peaches.

1. Preheat the broiler. Halve and pit the peaches, then lightly score the cut sides of each peach a few times with a knife.

2. Combine the liqueur and butter in a medium ovenproof skillet over medium heat; cook, stirring, until the butter melts and the liquid just begins to simmer. Add the peaches, cut-side up, and cook until the bottoms begin to soften, about 4 minutes. Sprinkle each peach half with 1 teaspoon sugar and transfer the skillet to the broiler. Broil until the peaches brown in spots, about 3 minutes. Let cool slightly.

3. Divide the peaches among plates and drizzle with the syrup from the skillet. Serve with the mascarpone.

Per serving: Calories 245; Fat 16 g (Saturated 9 g); Cholesterol 43 mg; Sodium 20 mg; Carbohydrate 20 g; Fiber 1 g; Protein 3 g

Balsamic Strawberries

Vegetarian | Gluten-Free

SERVES 6

ACTIVE: 15 min

TOTAL: 15 min

⅓ cup balsamic vinegar

2 tablespoons honey

1 bay leaf

Kosher salt

3 pints strawberries, quartered

2 cups vanilla low-fat Greek yogurt

The sweet-and-tangy balsamic reduction can be made several ahead; transfer to a small bowl, cover and refrigerate.

1. Combine the balsamic vinegar with the honey, bay leaf and a pinch of s a saucepan. Bring to a boil and cook until thick, about 4 minutes. Discard bay leaf; let the syrup cool.

2. Toss the strawberries with half of the balsamic syrup. Serve with the yogurt and the remaining balsamic syrup.

Per serving: Calories 128; Fat 2 g (Saturated 1 g); Cholesterol 5 mg; Sodium 71 mg; Carbohydrate 23 g; Fiber 3 g; Protein 7 g

Mango Sorbet with Coconut Sauce

Vegetarian | Vegan | Gluten-Free

SERVES 4

ACTIVE: 10 min

TOTAL: 10 min

1¼ cups light coconut milk

2 tablespoons packed dark brown sugar

6 fresh mint leaves

⅛ teaspoon cayenne pepper

Kosher salt

1 pint mango sorbet

Chopped pistachios, for topping

Stash some mango sorbet in your freezer: It tastes rich and creamy, and most brands are completely fat-free!

1. Combine the coconut milk, brown sugar, mint leaves, cayenne pepper and a pinch of salt in a blender and puree until smooth.

2. Scoop the mango sorbet into bowls, drizzle with the coconut sauce and top with chopped pistachios.

Per serving: Calories 213; Fat 6 g (Saturated 4 g); Cholesterol 0 mg; Sodium 93 mg; Carbohydrate 48 g; Fiber 1 g; Protein 2 g

Cherry Couscous Pudding

Vegetarian

SERVES 4

ACTIVE: 10 min

TOTAL: 20 min

1 cup skim milk

1 cup plain unsweetened almond milk

¼ cup sugar

¼ teaspoon almond extract

Pinch of kosher salt

¾ cup whole-wheat couscous

½ cup dried cherries

1 cinnamon stick

Toasted sliced almonds, for topping

Honey, for topping

Couscous doesn't sound like dessert, but in this recipe it tastes like rice pudding. Customize it with your favorite nuts and dried fruit.

1. Bring the skim milk, almond milk, sugar, almond extract and salt to a boil in a saucepan over medium heat. Add the couscous, dried cherries and cinnamon stick; cover and cook 2 minutes.

2. Remove from the heat and let sit, covered, until the couscous is tender, about 8 minutes. Fluff the couscous with a fork, remove the cinnamon stick and divide among bowls. Serve topped with almonds and honey.

Per serving: **Calories** 255; **Fat** 3 g (Saturated 0 g); **Cholesterol** 1 mg; **Sodium** 127 mg; **Carbohydrate** 53 g; **Fiber** 5 g; **Protein** 7 g

Broiled Apples with Jam

Vegetarian | Gluten-Free

SERVES 4

ACTIVE: 10 min

TOTAL: 10 min

- 4 Golden Delicious apples, quartered and cored
- 2 tablespoons unsalted butter, melted
- 3 to 4 tablespoons strawberry jam
- 1 pint vanilla frozen yogurt

Broiling these apples makes them extra sweet and tender. You can also try this recipe with pears.

1. Preheat the broiler. Arrange the apples, cut-side up, on a foil-lined baking sheet. Brush with the melted butter and broil until browned and slightly softened, about 5 minutes.

2. Brush or spoon the jam on the apples. Serve hot with the frozen yogurt.

Per serving: Calories 280; Fat 9 g (Saturated 5 g); Cholesterol 25 mg; Sodium 40 mg; Carbohydrate 52 g; Fiber 4 g; Protein 3 g

SNACK TIME!

Whip up a smoothie in seconds. Each makes 2 servings.

BLUEBERRY-BANANA
Blend 1 banana,
1 cup blueberries,
½ cup unsweetened
coconut milk, 1 tablespoon
each honey and lime juice,
¼ teaspoon almond
extract and 1 cup ice.

CREAMSICLE
Blend ¾ cup frozen orange or
orange-tangerine concentrate with
½ cup cold water and 1 cup each
vanilla frozen yogurt and ice.

RASPBERRY-ORANGE
Blend 1 cup each orange
juice and raspberries,
½ cup plain yogurt, 1 cup ice,
and sugar to taste.

HONEYDEW-ALMOND
Blend 2 cups chopped
honeydew melon, 1 cup
each almond milk and ice,
and honey to taste.

PINEAPPLE-COCONUT
Freeze about 2 cups coconut water in
1 or 2 ice-cube trays. Blend 2 cups each
chopped pineapple and coconut ice cubes,
1½ tablespoons lime juice, 1 tablespoon
honey and ½ cup coconut water.

POMEGRANATE-BERRY
Blend 1 cup blueberries,
¾ cup each beet juice and
pomegranate juice, 1 cup ice,
and honey to taste.

INDEX

INDEX